Murder on the Orient Express

AGATHA CHRISTIE

Level 4

Retold by Fiona Beddall
Series Editors: Andy Hopkins and Jocelyn Potter

Pearson Education Limited
Edinburgh Gate, Harlow,
Essex CM20 2JE, England
and Associated Companies throughout the world.

ISBN: 978-1-4058-9214-8

This edition first published by Pearson Education Ltd 2009

14

Set in 11/14pt Bembo
Printed in China
SWTC/14

The authors have asserted their moral rights in accordance with the
Copyright Designs and Patents Act 1988

Published by Pearson Education Ltd

Acknowledgements
We are grateful to the following for permission to reproduce their photographs:
Ronald Grant Archive: EMI Films: viii, 5, 8, 17, 21, 33, 35, 42, 48, 56, 67
All other images © Pearson Education

Every effort has been made to trace the copyright holders and we apologise in advance for
any unintentional omissions. We would be pleased to insert the appropriate
acknowledgement in any subsequent edition of this publication

For a complete list of the titles available in the Pearson English Readers series, please visit
www.pearsonenglishreaders.com. Alternatively, write to your local Pearson Education office
or to Pearson English Readers Marketing Department, Pearson Education, Edinburgh
Gate, Harlow, Essex CM20 2JE, England

Contents

Introduction

'To solve a case, a man just has to lie back in his chair and think.'

A train journey from Turkey to France is delayed by thick snow. When a passenger is found murdered in his bed, it is the perfect opportunity for Agatha Christie's famous private detective, Hercule Poirot, to prove his ability and solve the crime using the power of his brain.

Like all great murder mysteries, *Murder on the Orient Express* keeps us guessing until the final pages. Look for clues as you read, but be prepared for more than a few surprises!

Born in the town of Torquay in the south of England on 15 September 1890, Agatha Christie was the leading British writer of murder mysteries during her lifetime. She has continued to be popular since her death in 1976, and more copies of her books have been sold than of any other novelist in history. They have been translated into more than forty-five languages, and her play *The Mousetrap* has been on stage in London for more than fifty years without a break. How did the 'Queen of Crime' become so successful?

Her parents, a rich American businessman and his English wife, did not send Agatha to school as a child. She had a governess who taught her at home, allowing her to choose her own books and form her own ideas. She attended her first formal school at the age of sixteen, when she went to Paris to study singing and piano.

Although Agatha had not planned to be a writer, her writing skills were noticed at an early age. By the time she was eleven, one of her poems had been printed in the local newspaper. Before she was twenty several more of her poems had appeared in print and she had also written a number of short stories.

In 1914 the First World War began and Agatha married Colonel Archibald Christie. She worked in a hospital during the war, which gave her a knowledge of medicine that later proved useful in her work as a crime writer. The Christies' only child, Rosalind, was born in 1919. At about the same time, Agatha's sister Madge suggested that she should try to write a mystery novel.

The young writer decided that she needed a detective. At the time, her home town was full of Belgians who had been soldiers in the First World War, and Agatha decided that one of them would make the perfect model for Hercule Poirot. He starred in her first detective novel, *The Mysterious Affair at Styles* (1920), and later became the central character in thirty-three novels and fifty-four short stories.

Over the years Agatha Christie wrote about several different detectives, but Poirot had no equal in the hearts of her readers until she invented Miss Marple, who had much in common with her own grandmother. She did not plan to put Miss Marple into more than one book, but the public loved her and she eventually appeared in twelve Christie novels and twenty short stories.

Agatha Christie produced no fewer than sixty-six murder mystery novels, among the best of which are *The Murder of Roger Ackroyd* (1926), *Murder on the Orient Express* (1934) and *Death on the Nile* (1937). She also wrote several plays in addition to the record-breaking *The Mousetrap*, and six romantic novels using the name Mary Westmacott.

Agatha Christie's other great interest was travel. In the early 1920s she went round the world by sea with her first husband. After they separated in 1926, she continued to travel, alone and then with her second husband, Max Mallowan, who she married in 1930. She travelled several times on the Orient Express, which she described as 'the train of my dreams'.

Her enormous success was the result of a simple method: Christie wrote about the world that she knew. Working-class characters are rarely central to her stories, although plenty of servants appear; the books typically describe the lives of rich Englishmen and women like herself, and international tourists of the sort that she met on her travels. An idea for a new mystery could come into her head when she was taking a walk or shopping for a new hat; she filled piles of notebooks with ideas for stories and characters. She was, as her grandson Mathew Prichard has described her, '... a person who listened more than she talked, who saw more than she was seen.'

Murder on the Orient Express was written while Agatha Christie was staying in a hotel in Syria. It includes everything that her admirers like best in her stories: murder, confusing clues, a group of interesting characters, and a surprising solution by the clever detective, Hercule Poirot.

It is easy to understand why Christie's writing continues to entertain millions of readers around the world. The popularity of her stories goes beyond the printed page. There have been many television and film productions of *Murder on the Orient Express* and other Christie mysteries, and now there are video games too. Doubtless Agatha Christie's work will continue to excite readers and viewers for many, many years.

He looked quickly towards M. Poirot — at his enormous, curled moustache and strange, egg-shaped head — then looked away.

Chapter 1 The Journey Begins

The wonderful views of snow-topped mountains passed unnoticed as the train sped away from Syria towards Istanbul. As the Belgian detective M.* Hercule Poirot drank his coffee, he watched the only other person in the restaurant carriage – a tall, thin young lady, perhaps twenty-eight years old. From the way that she ate her breakfast, she seemed to be an experienced and confident traveller. He admired her pale face, tidy dark hair and cool grey eyes. A good-looking woman, he thought, but perhaps a little too cold and efficient to be described as pretty.

Soon a tall, thin man entered the restaurant carriage. He was between forty and fifty, with greying hair and skin darkened by the sun. He spoke to the woman. His accent was English.

'Morning, Miss Debenham.'

'Good morning, Colonel Arbuthnot,' she replied.

'Do you mind if I sit with you?'

'Of course not. Please, sit.' She smiled politely.

He sat down and ordered his breakfast. He looked quickly towards M. Poirot – at his enormous, curled moustache and strange, egg-shaped head – then looked away. 'Just a silly-looking foreigner,' he thought to himself.

The British pair exchanged a few polite words over their breakfast, and at lunchtime they sat together again. The man spoke of his life in the army in India, and occasionally asked the girl questions about Baghdad, where she had been a governess. When they discovered that they had some friends in common, they became more friendly.

'Are you stopping in Istanbul?' the man asked.

'No, I'm going straight through. I saw all the sights two years

* M.: short for *Monsieur*, the French word for Mr

ago, on my way to Baghdad.'

'Well, I must say I'm very glad about that. I'm going straight through too.' His face went a little red.

'That will be nice,' said Miss Debenham without emotion.

The train stopped late that evening at Konya. The two English travellers went outside for some fresh air and exercise. After a few minutes, Poirot decided to get some air too, and started to walk along the platform. It was bitterly cold.

Out of the darkness, he heard two voices. Arbuthnot was speaking. 'Mary –'

A girl interrupted him. 'Not now. Not now. When it's all over. When it's behind us – *then* –'

M. Poirot silently changed direction. 'Strange,' he said to himself. It was the voice of Miss Debenham, but a very different one from the cool, efficient voice that he had heard on the train.

The next afternoon, the train stopped unexpectedly. Poirot asked the conductor if there was a problem.

Miss Debenham was just behind him. 'What's the matter?' she asked Poirot in French. 'Why are we stopping?'

'Something caught fire under the restaurant carriage,' he explained, 'but they are repairing the damage. It is nothing serious.'

She looked impatient. 'But the *time*! This will delay us.'

'It is possible – yes,' agreed Poirot.

'But we can't afford delay! If we are delayed by more than an hour, we will miss our connection with the Orient* Express.'

Her hands were shaking. She was clearly very upset.

Luckily, her worries were soon forgotten. Ten minutes later the train was again on its way, and the rest of the journey to Istanbul went very smoothly. M. Poirot went straight to the Tokatlian Hotel. He was looking forward to a few days visiting

* Orient: a word used in the West to describe areas to the east and south-east

the sights in Istanbul before he continued his journey home.

At the hotel, he asked if he had any letters. There were three, and an urgent message too. This was a surprise.

'Unexpected change in Kassner case. Please return immediately,' he read.

'How annoying!' he said to himself. He looked at the clock.

'I must leave Istanbul tonight,' he told the man at the hotel desk. 'Can you get me a first-class compartment to London?'

'Of course, Monsieur. The train is almost empty in the winter. It leaves at nine o'clock.'

'Thank you,' said M. Poirot. He had just enough time for some dinner.

As he was ordering his food in the hotel restaurant, he felt a hand on his shoulder.

'M. Poirot! What an unexpected pleasure!' said a voice behind him. The speaker was a short, fat man in his fifties.

'M. Bouc!' cried Poirot.

M. Bouc was Belgian, and had a high position in the Compagnie Internationale des Wagons Lits*. The two men had been friends for many years, since the days when Poirot was a young detective in the Belgian police force.

'You are very far from home, my friend,' said M. Bouc.

'Yes. A little business in Syria. But I am heading home tonight – on the Orient Express, if there is a compartment.'

'Excellent! I will be on the same train. Later, you can tell me all your news. You are a famous detective now, I hear.'

With a warm smile, M. Bouc left the restaurant.

M. Poirot returned to the job of keeping his moustache out of the soup. Soon, though, his attention was caught by two men who were sitting together at a table not far from his. The younger

* Compagnie Internationale des Wagons Lits: a Belgian company that ran long-distance trains across Europe, starting in 1883 with the Orient Express

was a friendly-looking man of thirty, clearly an American. The other was in his sixties and seemed at first to be a kind old gentleman. But when his small, shadowy eyes met Poirot's, the detective's opinion of him changed completely. Just for a second Poirot sensed that the man was dangerous. It seemed that there was a wild animal hidden inside the man's body, looking out at the world with those evil eyes.

M. Poirot soon joined his friend M. Bouc near the hotel desk. Their conversation was interrupted by the hotel worker who was organising M. Poirot's train ticket.

'It is very strange, Monsieur. All the first-class compartments are booked – and the second-class too.'

'What?' asked M. Bouc. 'At this time of year? Impossible!'

'But it is true, sir,' the man replied. 'I am sorry.'

'Well, well,' M. Bouc said to Poirot, 'do not worry. We will arrange something with the conductor.' He looked up at the clock. 'Come,' he said, 'it is time to go.'

At the station, M. Bouc took the conductor to one side.

'We must find a compartment for this gentleman here. He is a friend of mine.'

'But we are completely full, Monsieur. It is most unusual.'

'Well,' said M. Bouc, 'tomorrow there will be more compartments, when we reach Belgrade. The problem is for tonight.' He paused for a moment. 'Everyone has arrived?'

The conductor looked at his list. 'Number 7 – a second-class compartment. The gentleman – a Mr Harris – has not yet come, and it is four minutes to nine.'

'Then put M. Poirot's luggage in number 7,' said M. Bouc. 'If this Mr Harris arrives, we will tell him that he is too late.'

With words of thanks to M. Bouc, Poirot followed his luggage to compartment 7. Inside it was the tall young American from the hotel.

He was not pleased when Poirot entered. 'Excuse me,' he said

'We must find a compartment for this gentleman here.
He is a friend of mine.'

in French. 'I think you've made a mistake.'

'There are no other beds on the train, M. MacQueen,' the conductor apologised. 'The gentleman has to come in here.'

Poirot noticed that the conductor seemed almost as annoyed as the American. Perhaps he had been offered money to keep the other bed empty.

When the conductor had left, MacQueen's annoyance seemed forgotten.

'The train's surprisingly full,' he said with a smile.

Just then, the train started moving. Their three-day journey across Europe had begun.

After a good night's sleep, Poirot spent the morning alone in his compartment, looking at his notes on the case that had called him to London.

He had a late lunch with M. Bouc. As they relaxed at the end of the meal, they looked around the restaurant carriage.

'If I were a writer, I would use this scene,' said M. Bouc. 'All around us are people of all classes, of all nationalities, of all ages. For three days these people sleep and eat under one roof. They cannot escape each other. But at the end of the three days they go their separate ways and never see each other again.'

There were thirteen people in the restaurant carriage, and M. Bouc was right: they were a very mixed group. A big, hairy Italian was sitting with a thin, pale Englishman, probably a servant, and an American in a brightly-coloured suit. The American and Italian exchanged business advice while the Englishman stared out of the window. He was clearly not enjoying the conversation.

At the next table sat an ugly lady whose clothes and jewellery, though they did nothing to help her appearance, were clearly from the most expensive shops in Paris.

'That is Princess Dragomiroff,' said M. Bouc. 'She is Russian, but her husband got his money out of the country before the Communists took control. So ugly, but what a character!'

At another table, Mary Debenham was sitting with a kind-looking middle-aged woman with fair hair and a sheep-like face; with them was an older woman, an American who never seemed to stop talking. Colonel Arbuthnot was at the next table, alone. Against the wall sat a middle-aged woman dressed in black — a servant, Poirot guessed. Then there was a good-looking man of about thirty with a beautiful young woman. Perfectly dressed in the latest fashion, she had pale skin and large brown eyes. Poirot could not take his eyes off her.

'A Hungarian diplomat and his wife, I believe,' said M. Bouc, seeing his friend's interest. 'A very attractive couple.'

Then there was MacQueen and his employer, the man with the kind face and the small, cruel eyes.

M. Bouc returned to his compartment while M. Poirot finished his coffee.

'My daughter said I would have no trouble with these food

tickets,' he heard the American woman say to Miss Debenham as she paid the waiter. 'But then there's money for the waiter, and that bottle of water. Nasty water too. They haven't got any Evian, which seems very odd to me.' She looked crossly at the coins in front of her. 'And look at this rubbish that the waiter's given me. *Dinars** or something. My daughter said –'

At this point, Mary Debenham made a polite excuse and left the table. Colonel Arbuthnot got up and followed her. Very soon the restaurant carriage was empty except for Poirot and MacQueen's employer.

To the detective's surprise, the man came and sat down at his table. 'Good afternoon,' he said in a quiet, deep voice. 'My name is Ratchett. I think that I have the pleasure of speaking to Mr Hercule Poirot. Is that right?'

'Your information is correct, Monsieur,' said the detective.

'I want you to do a job for me,' said Ratchett.

Poirot looked surprised. 'I take very few cases, I'm afraid.'

'Of course. But this, Mr Poirot, means money. *Big* money.'

Poirot was silent for a moment. Then he said, 'What do you wish me to do for you, M. – er – Ratchett?'

'Mr Poirot, I am a rich man – a very rich man. Men in my position have enemies. Someone has threatened to kill me. I can look after myself quite well.' He quickly showed Poirot the gun in his pocket. 'But I'd like to be especially careful. Remember, we are talking big money, Mr Poirot.'

Poirot thought for some minutes. Finally he said, 'I am sorry, Monsieur, but I cannot help you.'

The other man smiled. 'Not even if I give you twenty thousand dollars?'

'No, Monsieur.'

* dinar: a form of money that used to be used in countries like Serbia that were part of Yugoslavia

Poirot stood up. 'Forgive me for being personal,
but I do not like your face, M. Ratchett.'

'But why not? Why does this case not interest you?'

Poirot stood up. 'Forgive me for being personal, but I do not like your face, M. Ratchett,' he said.

The Orient Express arrived at Belgrade at a quarter to nine that evening. M. Bouc was moved into a carriage that had just joined the train from Athens, and Poirot was given M. Bouc's old compartment, number 1. At 9.15, with heavy snow falling outside, the train was on its way again.

The strangers of yesterday were already becoming more friendly. Colonel Arbuthnot was standing at the door of his compartment talking to MacQueen.

Two doors from Poirot's new compartment, the older American woman, Mrs Hubbard, was talking to the sheep-like lady.

'Oh, isn't this cold weather terrible! I hope your head will be better in the morning. Have you got some aspirin? Are you sure? I've got plenty. Well, good night, my dear.'

She turned to Poirot as the other woman departed.

'Poor woman, she's Swedish. Some kind of teacher. Very nice, but doesn't talk much English. She was very interested to hear about my daughter.'

Poirot, like everyone else on the train, now knew all about Mrs Hubbard's daughter, who was teaching at a big American college in Turkey. They also knew Mrs Hubbard's opinion of Turks, their lazy habits and the terrible condition of their roads.

The door next to them opened and the thin, pale manservant came out. Inside, Poirot saw Mr Ratchett sitting up in bed. Then the door was shut.

Mrs Hubbard moved closer to Poirot.

'You know, I'm frightened of that man,' she said quietly. 'Not the servant – the other man. I can just feel that he's dangerous. He's next door to me and I don't like it. It wouldn't surprise me if he was a murderer.'

Colonel Arbuthnot and MacQueen were coming towards them down the corridor. 'Come into my compartment,' MacQueen was saying, 'and we can talk some more. So you think that in India the British should –'

The voice suddenly went quiet as the two men entered MacQueen's compartment.

'I'm going to bed,' Mrs Hubbard said to Poirot. 'Good night.'

Poirot went into his own compartment, which was the next one beyond Ratchett's. He read in bed for about half an hour and then turned out the light.

He was woken a few hours later by a cry. It sounded like a cry of pain, from somewhere not far away. This was immediately followed by the ringing of a bell.

Poirot sat up and switched on the light. He noticed that the train was not moving. Remembering that Ratchett was in the next-door compartment, he got out of bed and opened the door. The conductor was hurrying along the corridor. He knocked on

Ratchett's door. No answer. He knocked a second time, just as another bell rang further down the corridor and a light was turned on. From Ratchett's compartment, a voice called out, '*Ce n'est rien. Je me suis trompé.*'

'Very good, Monsieur,' said the conductor. He hurried off again, towards the door where the light was showing.

Poirot returned to bed, checked his watch and switched off the light. It was twenty-three minutes to one.

He could not sleep. The noises on board the train seemed unusually loud. He could hear Ratchett moving around next door, and footsteps in the corridor outside.

His throat felt dry. He had forgotten to ask for his usual bottle of water. He looked at his watch again. A quarter past one. He was thinking of ringing for the conductor and asking him for water when he heard another bell ring. *Ting ... ting ... ting ...*

Poirot waited. The conductor could not come to two compartments at the same time.

The bell sounded again and again. Someone was clearly getting impatient. Finally the conductor came. Poirot heard him apologise. Then there was a woman's voice – Mrs Hubbard's. She spoke for some time, with the conductor adding a few words here and there. Then the conductor said goodnight and the door was closed.

Poirot took his chance and rang his own bell. The conductor, when he came, looked upset. 'It is Mrs Hubbard,' he explained. 'She says that there is a man in her room. Imagine it – in a room of that size! Where could he hide? I told her that it was impossible, but she didn't listen. We have enough to worry about already, with this snow –'

'Snow?'

'Yes, Monsieur. There is too much snow on the line. The

★ *Ce n'est rien. Je me suis trompé.*: French for 'It is nothing, I made a mistake.'

train has stopped. We might have to wait here for days.'

He brought Poirot the water, then said goodnight.

Poirot drank a glass of water and began to fall asleep. He was soon wide awake again, though. There had been a loud noise from the next-door compartment. Had something heavy fallen against the door? He jumped out of bed and looked out. Nothing, except a woman in a red dressing gown some distance down the corridor. At the other end of the corridor, the conductor was doing some paperwork. Everything was quiet.

'I should stop worrying,' he said to himself, and went back to bed. This time he slept until morning.

Chapter 2   A Cruel and Dangerous Man

When Poirot woke, the train was still not moving. There was deep snow all around them. In the restaurant carriage, everyone was complaining about the delay.

'How long will we be here?' Mary Debenham asked. 'Doesn't anybody *know*?'

Her voice sounded impatient, but she was not upset in the way that she had been at the delay before reaching Istanbul.

Mrs Hubbard replied, 'Nobody knows anything on this train, and nobody's trying to do anything. If this was in America, people would at least *try* to do something! My daughter says –'

The morning continued in this way. Poirot learnt a lot more about Mrs Hubbard's daughter and about the habits of Mr Hubbard, who had recently died.

Turning round, Poirot noticed a conductor at his elbow – not the conductor from the night before, but a big, fair man.

'Excuse me, Monsieur,' he said. 'M. Bouc would be grateful if you could come to him for a few minutes.'

Poirot made his excuses to the ladies and followed the

conductor to a compartment in the next carriage. M. Bouc was sitting there with a small, dark man, and a man in a blue uniform – the train manager. The conductor from the night before was standing by the window.

'My good friend,' cried M. Bouc, 'we need your help!'

M. Bouc was clearly upset. Poirot realised at once that the matter was serious. 'What has happened?' he asked.

'Well, first this terrible snow – this delay. And now –'

He stopped.

'And now what?'

'And now a passenger lies murdered in his bed.'

'Which passenger?' asked M. Poirot.

'An American. A man called – called –' M. Bouc looked at his notes. 'Ratchett. It is a disaster! A murder is bad enough. But the train cannot move. We may be here for days. We have no police on board, and Dr Constantine thinks that the murderer is still among us.'

The small, dark man now spoke. 'The window of M. Ratchett's compartment was found wide open, but there were no footprints in the snow. No one left the train that way.'

'At what time was the murder?' asked the detective.

'It is difficult to give an exact time,' replied the doctor, 'but it was some time between midnight and 2 a.m.'

'And the crime was discovered – when?'

M. Bouc turned to Michel, the conductor by the window, who looked pale and frightened.

'The waiter from the restaurant carriage wanted to know if Monsieur wanted lunch,' said the conductor. 'There was no answer. I opened the door with my key, but there was a bolt too. I called the train manager. We cut through the bolt and went in. He was – it was terrible. Terrible!' He hid his face in his hands.

'The door was locked and bolted on the inside,' said Poirot thoughtfully. 'Perhaps he killed himself?'

'Does a man kill himself with twelve knife wounds in the chest?' asked the doctor.

'It was a woman,' said the train manager, speaking for the first time. 'Only a woman would kill like that.'

'Then it was a very strong woman,' said the doctor. 'The knife went through bone in some places.'

'So, my friend, you see our problem.' M. Bouc looked at the detective. 'Can you help us?'

'What exactly do you want me to do?' M. Poirot asked.

'Take command of the case! When the police arrive, there will be problems, delays, unpleasantness. It would be so much better if the case was already solved when they arrived. And you are the perfect man for the job. Examine the body and interview the passengers. You will not be able to check their stories, but you once said, "To solve a case, a man just has to lie back in his chair and think." Do that – and you will know!'

'I accept the case willingly,' smiled the detective. 'It will help to pass the time.'

'Wonderful!' said M. Bouc. 'We will help you in any way that we can.'

'First, I would like a plan of the carriage where the murder took place, with a note of the names of the people in each compartment. I will also need their passports and tickets.'

'Michel will get you those.'

The conductor left the compartment.

'Who are the other passengers on the train?' asked M. Poirot.

'In this carriage, Dr Constantine and I are the only travellers. Behind this are the third-class carriages, but they were locked after dinner last night. In front, there is only the restaurant carriage.'

'So it seems likely that the murderer is now in the American's carriage,' said Poirot.

'Yes,' agreed Dr Constantine. 'At half past midnight we were stopped by the snow. No one has left the train since then – or at least, there are certainly no footprints in the snow.'

'First I would like to speak with young M. MacQueen,' said Poirot. 'He may be able to give us some useful information.'

The train manager fetched MacQueen.

'What's the problem?' asked the American nervously as he sat down opposite Poirot. 'Has anything happened?'

'Yes, Monsieur,' answered the detective. 'Prepare yourself for a shock. Your employer, M. Ratchett, has been murdered.'

MacQueen's eyes seemed brighter, but except for this he showed no signs of shock. 'So they got him after all,' he said.

'What do you mean, M. MacQueen?'

MacQueen paused. 'And you are –?'

'I am a detective working for the Compagnie Internationale des Wagons Lits. My name is M. Hercule Poirot. Now, please, tell me what you mean, *They got him after all.*'

'Well, he has been getting letters. Threatening letters.'

'Did you see them?'

'Yes. I am – was – his secretary. It was my job to answer his letters. The first came last week. Would you like to see it?'

'Yes, that would be most helpful,' replied the detective.

MacQueen left, and soon returned with a rather dirty piece of notepaper. Poirot read the carefully printed handwriting:

You thought you could cheat us, didn't you? Well, you were wrong. We're going to get you, Ratchett!

'And the other letters were similar?' asked the detective.

'Yes, very similar. Ratchett pretended to laugh about them, but I could see that they worried him.'

'How long have you been working for M. Ratchett?'

'A year. He travelled around a lot, but he spoke no languages except English. I was more his translator than his secretary.'

'Now, tell me as much as you can about your employer.'

'That's not so easy.' He looked confused.

'He was an American citizen?'

'Yes.'

'What part of America was he from?'

'I don't know. I know almost nothing about him. Mr Ratchett never spoke of himself, or his family, or his life in America.'

'Why was that, do you think?'

'Well, I think he was hiding something – something in his past. I'm not even sure that Ratchett was his real name.'

'One last question. Did you have a good relationship with your employer?'

'Well, yes, I did. I didn't like him very much as a person, but I had no problems with him as an employer.'

'You did not like him. Why was that?'

'I can't exactly say.' He paused, then continued, 'He was, I am sure, a cruel and dangerous man. I have no reason for this opinion, M. Poirot, but I feel it very strongly.'

'Thank you for your honesty, Mr MacQueen.'

M. Poirot and Dr Constantine went together to the compartment of the murdered man. It was freezing cold inside. The window was pushed down as far as it could go.

'I did not like to close it,' said the doctor. 'Nothing has been touched in here, and I was careful not to move the body when I examined it.'

'Good,' said Poirot. He checked the window for fingerprints, but there were none. 'Criminals these days are always careful about fingerprints. And you were right, Doctor. There are no footprints in the snow. No one left the carriage through this window – although perhaps the murderer wanted us to think that he did.'

Poirot closed the window and turned his attention to the body. Ratchett was lying on his back in the bed. The detective bent down to look at the wounds.

'How many wounds are there exactly?' he asked.

'Twelve, I think. Some are very slight, but at least three are serious enough to cause death. And there is something strange. These two wounds – here and here –' He pointed. 'They are deep, but they have not bled in the normal way.'

'Which means –?

'That the man was already dead – dead for some time – when these wounds were made. But that seems impossible.'

'Unlikely, certainly – unless our murderer was worried that he hadn't done the job right the first time and came back to make sure.' He paused, then asked suddenly, 'Were the lights on?'

'No,' replied the doctor.

Poirot thought for a moment. 'So we have two murderers. The first did his job, then turned off the light as he left. Later, the second arrived in the dark, did not see that his or her work had been done and struck at a dead body. What do you think?'

'Very good!' said the doctor. 'That would also explain why some wounds are deep but others are so slight. We have a strong murderer and a weaker one.'

'Yes, but two independent murderers on the same night? It is so *unlikely*!' Poirot stopped, then continued, 'Could the deepest wounds be the work of a woman?'

'Perhaps – but only if she was very strong.'

Poirot put his hand under the pillow and pulled out the gun that Ratchett had shown him the day before. 'Why didn't the American defend himself? The bullets are all there, you see.'

They looked round the room. Ratchett's clothes were hanging tidily behind the door. On a small table was a bottle of water, an empty glass, some burnt pieces of paper and a used match.

The doctor picked up the empty glass and smelled it. 'This is why Ratchett failed to defend himself. He was drugged.'

Poirot felt in Ratchett's pockets and soon brought out a box of matches. He compared the matches carefully with the one on the table. 'The match on the table is a different shape from these – shorter and flatter. Perhaps it was the murderer's.'

The detective continued to look round the room. Then, with a cry, he bent down and picked up a handkerchief from the floor. It was small and pretty.

'The train manager was right!' he said. 'There is a woman in this case. And she very conveniently leaves us a clue – exactly as it happens in the books and films. And to make things even easier for us, there is a letter H on it.'

Poirot made another dive to the floor, and this time stood up with a pipe cleaner in his hand. 'Another convenient clue,' he smiled. 'And this time it suggests a man, not a woman.'

The doctor was now looking in the front pocket of Ratchett's pyjamas. 'Ah!' he said. 'I didn't notice this earlier.'

He showed Poirot a gold pocket watch. The case was badly damaged, and the hands pointed to a quarter past one.

'You see?' cried Constantine. 'This gives us the hour of the

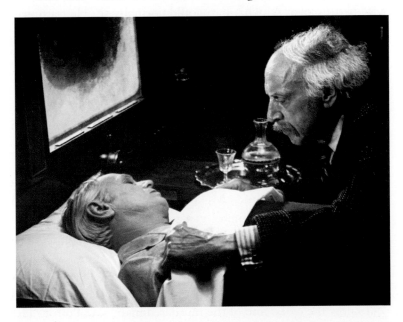

The doctor was now looking in the front pocket of Ratchett's pyjamas.

crime. It fits perfectly with the medical evidence, that he died between midnight and 2 a.m.'

'It is possible, yes,' said the detective in a troubled voice.

He went back to the little table and examined the burnt bits of paper. 'I need a ladies' hat box!' he said softly.

Before Dr Constantine was able to ask why, Poirot was in the corridor, calling for the conductor. The conductor soon came in with a hat box borrowed from one of the lady passengers.

'There are so many clues in this room,' Poirot explained to the doctor, who was looking very confused. 'The watch, the pipe cleaner, the handkerchief. But how can we be sure that they are not false clues, left here to confuse us? I am only sure of two clues – the match and the burnt paper. The murderer didn't want us to read the words on that paper. Let us see.'

From the hat box, Poirot took one of the pieces of shaped wire netting over which a hat would normally sit. He flattened it, then carefully placed the burnt pieces of paper on top and covered them with another piece of wire netting. He lit a match and held the wire over the flame. The doctor watched with interest as, slowly, some words appeared – words of fire.

'–member little Daisy Armstrong.'

'Ah!' cried Poirot. 'So Ratchett was not the dead man's real name. We now know his name, and why he left America.'

'We do?' asked the doctor.

'Yes. We must go and tell M. Bouc.'

The two men found M. Bouc finishing lunch in his compartment. 'After lunch, we will empty the restaurant carriage and use it for your interviews,' M. Bouc said. 'I have ordered some food for you here.'

The doctor and the detective ate quickly. M. Bouc waited until their coffee had been served, then asked, 'Well?'

'I know the real name of the murdered man,' said Poirot. 'He was Cassetti. Do you remember the Armstrong case?'

'Yes, I think I do,' answered M. Bouc. 'A terrible business – although I cannot remember the details.'

'Colonel Armstrong was an Englishman, married to the daughter of America's most famous actress, Linda Arden. They were living in America when their three-year-old daughter was kidnapped. After messages from the kidnappers, the parents paid them more than two hundred thousand dollars for her return. But instead, the child's dead body was discovered. Mrs Armstrong was carrying another baby at the time, and the shock of her daughter's murder made her give birth too soon. She and the baby both died. The heartbroken husband then shot himself.'

'Yes, I remember now,' M. Bouc said softly. 'And there was another death too, wasn't there?'

'A French or Swiss girl who worked for the Armstrongs. The police believed that she had helped the kidnappers, although she strongly denied this. She threw herself out of a window. Later, it was proved that she was completely innocent.'

'Terrible!' said the doctor.

'About six months after these events, the police caught Cassetti. He was the leader of a team of gangsters who had kidnapped and killed people in a similar way before. There was no doubt that he was guilty of the Armstrong kidnap too. But Cassetti was very rich, and he used his money to escape punishment for his crimes. After the court case, he disappeared. And now we know where he went. He changed his name to Ratchett and began travelling abroad.'

'What an animal!' cried M. Bouc. 'He got what he deserved.'

'I agree,' said M. Poirot. 'But was the murderer another gangster, or someone connected to Daisy Armstrong?'

'Are there any members of the Armstrong family living?'

'I don't know,' replied the detective. 'I seem to remember that Mrs Armstrong had a younger sister.'

There was a knock at the door. 'The restaurant carriage is ready for you, Monsieur,' said the waiter to M. Bouc.

The three men walked down the corridor to begin the interviews.

Chapter 3   A Red Dressing Gown and a Metal Button

In the restaurant carriage, everything was ready – a pile of passports and tickets, a plan of the carriage with the names of the passengers marked on it, and writing paper, a pen and ink.

'Excellent,' said Poirot. 'Our first interview will be with the conductor. You probably know something about his character, M. Bouc. Should we believe his evidence?'

'Definitely,' replied M. Bouc. 'Pierre Michel has worked for the company for fifteen years. A Frenchman – very honest.'

Michel entered the carriage. He seemed less upset than he had been earlier, but he was still very nervous.

'Now, Michel,' said M. Poirot gently, 'we have to ask you a few things about last night. M. Ratchett went to bed – when?'

'Soon after dinner, Monsieur – before we left Belgrade.'

'Did you see anyone go into his compartment afterwards?'

'His manservant, Monsieur, and his secretary. No one else.'

'And was that the last time you saw or heard from him?'

'No, Monsieur. He rang his bell at about twenty to one. I knocked, but he called out, '*Ce n'est rien. Je me suis trompé.*'

'And where were you at a quarter past one?'

'Most of the time I was at my seat at the end of the corridor. Soon after one – I don't know when exactly – I went to the next carriage to talk to a colleague about the snow. Then Mrs Hubbard rang, and I spoke to her for a few minutes. Then I brought you some water, Monsieur.'

He seemed less upset than he had been earlier, but he was still very nervous.

'And later?'

'At about two o'clock M. MacQueen asked me to make his bed. The English Colonel from number 15 was there with him. When they had gone to bed, I sat at my seat until morning.'

'Did you sleep?'

'I don't think so, Monsieur.'

'Did you see any of the passengers in the corridor?'

The conductor thought for a moment. 'One of the ladies went to the toilet.'

'Which one?'

'I don't know, but she was wearing a red dressing gown. It had a Chinese-style picture on the back.'

'And after that?'

'You yourself opened the door and looked out for a second.'

'Good,' said Poirot. 'I wondered if you would remember that. Now, if the murderer came onto the train last night –'

'There were no strangers on the train last night, Monsieur. The door to the next carriage was bolted on the inside. I opened the side door when we stopped at Vincovci at twenty past twelve, but I was standing there all the time. No one came through it.'

'What about the side door beyond the restaurant carriage?'

'That is always bolted on the inside at night.'

'It isn't bolted now.'

The man looked surprised for a moment. 'Perhaps one of the passengers opened it to look at the snow,' he said finally. 'Monsieur, you do not blame me?'

Poirot smiled at him kindly. 'Of course not, my friend. Ah! I have one other thing to ask you. Another bell rang just after you knocked on M. Ratchett's door. Whose was it?'

'Princess Dragomiroff's, Monsieur. She wanted her maid.'

'You called the maid?'

'Yes, Monsieur.'

'That is all. Thank you for your help.'

The conductor left the restaurant carriage and Poirot called Mr MacQueen for another interview.

When MacQueen learnt that his employer had been the criminal Cassetti, he was very angry. 'How terrible that I helped an evil man like that!' he cried.

'You seem to feel very strongly about this, M. MacQueen.'

'Yes, I do. My father was on the legal team in the Armstrong case. He knew that Cassetti was guilty, but things went wrong in court and it couldn't be proved. Well, I'm glad that he's dead – although I didn't kill him myself, you understand.'

'Of course, of course. Now, I must check the movements of everyone on the train. What did you do last night after dinner?'

'Well, I talked to some of the other passengers. At about ten o'clock, I went into Mr Ratchett's compartment and he asked me to write some letters for him. Then I got into a long conversation with Colonel Arbuthnot.'

'Do you know what time you went to bed?'

'About two o'clock, I think.'

'Did you leave the train at any time?'

'Arbuthnot and I got out at – what was the name of the place? – Vincovci. But it was bitterly cold, so we soon came back in.'

'By which door did you leave the train?'

'By the one next to the restaurant carriage.'

'Do you remember if it was bolted?'

MacQueen stopped to think. 'Yes, I believe it was.'

'And did you bolt it again when you got back on the train?'

'I got on last, and no, I don't think I bolted it.'

'When you were with Colonel Arbuthnot,' continued the detective, 'the door of your compartment was open, I think. Please tell me who passed along the corridor after the train left Vincovci.'

'The conductor – and a woman too, going towards the restaurant carriage.'

'Which woman?'

'I don't know. I just remember seeing a thin red dressing gown. She was probably going to the toilet.'

'Did you see her return?'

'Well, no, I don't remember seeing her.'

'One more question. Do you smoke a pipe?'

'No, sir, I don't,' replied MacQueen.

'I think that is all at present. Thank you for your time. I would now like to speak to M. Ratchett's manservant.'

The American left and the thin, pale Englishman arrived. The detective picked up his passport.

'You are the manservant of M. Ratchett – Edward Henry Masterman, age thirty-nine, a British citizen?'

'Yes, sir.'

'You have heard that your employer has been murdered?'

'Yes, sir. A terrible crime.'

'Please tell me when you last saw M. Ratchett.'

'It was at about nine o'clock last night, sir. I went to Mr Ratchett as usual, and helped him to get ready for bed.'

'What sort of mood was he in?'

'Not a good one, sir. He had just read a letter and I think he was upset about it. He criticised everything that I did.'

'Was that unusual?'

'No, sir. He lost his temper easily.'

'Did M. Ratchett ever take any medicine to help him sleep?'

Dr Constantine moved forward a little to hear his answer.

'Always, sir, when he was travelling. He said that he could not sleep without it.'

'Did he take it last night?'

'Yes, sir. I poured it into a glass for him myself.'

'Did you like your employer, M. Masterman?'

The manservant's face showed no emotion. 'He paid me well, sir – but I'm not very fond of Americans.'

'Have you ever been to America?'

'No, sir.'

'And what did you do after leaving M. Ratchett last night?'

'I told Mr MacQueen that he was wanted. Then I went back to my own compartment and read.'

'You were in compartment number 4.'

'Yes, sir, with a big Italian man.'

'Does the Italian speak English?'

'Well, a kind of English, sir. He's been in America – Chicago, I understand. We do not talk much. I prefer to read.'

'What time did you go to sleep?'

'I went to *bed* at about ten thirty, sir, but I didn't sleep. I had toothache.'

'Did you not sleep at all?'

'Yes, in the end. But not until about four in the morning.'

'Did you leave your compartment during the night?'

'No, sir.'

'And the Italian?'

'No, sir. He slept all night.'

'One last question. Do you smoke a pipe?'

'No, sir. I only smoke cigarettes.'

'Thank you, Mr Masterman. I think that is all.'

'Excuse me, sir, but the American lady, Mrs Hubbard, says she knows all about the murderer. She is very upset, sir.'

'Then we should see her next, I think,' said Poirot, smiling.

Mrs Hubbard entered the restaurant carriage talking excitedly.

'Now who's in charge here, because I have some very important information. *Very* important.'

'Please, Madame*, sit,' said Poirot. 'Then tell me everything.'

'Well, I will tell you *this*. There was a murder on the train last night, and the murderer was *in my compartment!*'

'You are sure of this, Madame?'

'Of course I'm sure! I was asleep, and suddenly I woke up. It was dark – and I knew that there was a man in my compartment. I was so frightened that I couldn't scream. I thought, "I'm going to be killed!" It was so terrible – these nasty trains, and the horrible things that happen on them! And then I thought, "Well, he won't get my jewellery," because I'd hidden it under my pillow. Very uncomfortable, I can tell you. But that's not important. Where was I?'

'You realised that there was a man in your compartment.'

'Yes, well, I just lay there with my eyes closed for some time. Then I felt for the bell with my hand and pressed it to call the conductor. I rang and rang, but nothing happened. "Maybe they've already murdered everyone else on the train," I thought. Then finally the conductor came in. I switched on the lights, *but*

* Madame: French for Mrs or madam

25

there wasn't anyone there at all.'

Judging by Mrs Hubbard's voice, she thought that her last words were the most exciting part of her story.

'And what happened next, Madame?'

'Well, I told the conductor what had happened, and he didn't seem to believe me. Clearly the man had got away, but the conductor only wanted to calm me down! Well, at the time I was worried that the man was the one from the next-door compartment. I asked the conductor to look at the door between the compartments, and of course it wasn't bolted. Well, I bolted it immediately, and put a suitcase against it too.'

'And do you think the man in your compartment went into Mr Ratchett's compartment, or out into the corridor?'

'How could I know that? My eyes were tight shut. Oh, if my daughter knew how frightened I was!'

'Perhaps, Madame, you heard someone not in your own compartment but in the compartment of the murdered man.'

'Certainly not! And I can prove it!'

From her handbag, she produced a small metal button.

'You see this? I found it this morning in my compartment.'

As she placed the button on the table, M. Bouc cried, 'This is a button from a conductor's uniform!'

'It probably fell off Michel's uniform when he was helping Madame Hubbard last night,' said Poirot.

'Why don't you people believe me?' cried the American woman. 'At bedtime last night I was reading a magazine. When I switched off the light, I put the magazine on the floor near the window. Last night, after the man had been in my room, the conductor went nowhere near the window, but in the morning the button was on top of the magazine. What do you call that?'

'I call that evidence, Madame,' replied the detective seriously. 'Now, can I ask you a few questions?'

'Of course,' said Mrs Hubbard.

'You were nervous of this man Ratchett. So why had you not already bolted the door between the compartments?'

'I had. Or at least, I had asked that Swedish lady if it was bolted, and she had said that it was.'

'Why couldn't you see for yourself?'

'I was in bed and my sponge bag was hanging on the door handle.'

'When was this?'

'About half past ten, I think. The Swedish lady had come to ask me for an aspirin.'

'Do you remember the case of the Armstrong kidnap?'

'Of course I do. I didn't know the Armstrongs personally. They moved in higher society than I. But I've always heard that they were a lovely couple. Oh, that evil man Cassetti –'

'Ratchett was Cassetti,' said Poirot.

'Cassetti, on this train! I can't believe it! I must tell my daughter.'

'Now, Madame, just one more thing. Do you have a red dressing gown?'

'What an odd question! No, I don't.'

Poirot helped her towards the door. At the last moment he said, 'You have dropped your handkerchief, Madame.'

She looked at the little piece of material that he was holding out to her. 'That isn't mine. It's much too small – mine are a sensible size.'

'Ah!' said the detective. 'It had an H on it. I thought it must be yours.'

Chapter 4 An Open Door

As Mrs Hubbard left, M. Bouc said anxiously, 'I hope this button doesn't mean that Pierre Michel is the murderer.'

'That button is interesting,' said Poirot. 'But let us interview the Swedish lady before we discuss it.' He looked through the pile of passports. 'Here we are. Greta Ohlsson, age forty-nine.'

M. Bouc asked the waiter to invite her in. The woman with a sheep-like face and fair hair entered. She looked quite calm.

'You know what happened last night?' asked Poirot.

'Yes. It is terrible,' she replied.

'You will understand, Mademoiselle*, that I must ask everyone about their movements last night after dinner.'

'Of course. Well, I spent most of the evening in my compartment, but I did go to see the American lady, Mrs Hubbard. She gave me some aspirin.'

'Did she ask if the door between her compartment and Mr Ratchett's was bolted?'

'Yes, she did. And it was.'

'And after that?'

'I went back to my bed, took the aspirin and fell asleep.'

'Your compartment is this one?' He pointed to the plan.

'Yes, I think so. I am sharing with a young English lady. Very nice. She has travelled from Baghdad.'

'Did she leave the compartment during the night?'

'No, I am sure she did not.'

'Why are you sure if you were asleep?'

'I wake very easily. She was sleeping in the bed above mine. I always notice when she comes down.'

'Did *you* leave the compartment?'

'Not until this morning.'

'Do you have a red dressing gown?'

'No, I do not. Mine is brown.'

'Have you ever been to America, Mademoiselle?'

'Sadly, no. I like the Americans. They give a lot of money to

* Mademoiselle: the French word for Miss

28

schools and hospitals in Turkey. Why do you ask?'

Poirot explained about the Armstrong case. Greta Ohlsson left the interview room shaking her head and crying, 'How can there be such evil in the world?'

Poirot spent some time writing notes. 'The conductor said that Mrs Hubbard's bell rang some time after 1 a.m.'

'Yes, it seems quite clear that the murder happened at 1.15,' said M. Bouc. 'That fits the evidence of the watch and the stories of the conductor and Mrs Hubbard. And I think I can guess who the murderer is. It is the big Italian. Italians always kill with a knife, and this one has lived in America. He and Ratchett probably worked in this kidnapping business together. Then Ratchett cheated him. The Italian wanted revenge. He sent threatening letters and then he killed him. Very simple.'

'Simple except for the manservant with the toothache, who says that the Italian never left the compartment,' said Poirot.

'Yes, that is a difficulty, but it will all be explained,' said M. Bouc confidently.

The detective shook his head. 'No, it is not as simple as that, I fear. But let us hear what Pierre Michel can tell us about this button.'

The conductor was called and shown the button.

'It seems certain,' said M. Bouc, 'that the murderer passed through Mrs Hubbard's compartment and dropped that button.'

Michel was very upset. 'It is not mine, Monsieur! Look – my uniform has lost no buttons. I am innocent of this crime!'

'Where were you when Mrs Hubbard's bell rang?'

'In the next carriage, Monsieur. I was talking to a colleague.'

The colleague was called. His story agreed with Michel's. The buttons of all the other conductors' uniforms were checked, and none were missing.

'Monsieur, do you see now? I am not guilty!' cried Michel.

'Calm yourself, Michel,' said M. Bouc. 'Think back to last

night. When you ran to answer Mrs Hubbard's bell, did you see anyone in the corridor?'

'No, Monsieur.'

'That is no surprise,' said Poirot. 'Mrs Hubbard lay with her eyes closed for some time after she realised that there was someone in her compartment. The man probably went out then. If the murderer was one of the passengers, he had time to get back to his own compartment before Michel arrived.'

'We still have eight passengers to interview,' said M. Bouc. 'Shall we see the Italian next?'

'You think only of your Italian!' laughed Poirot. 'No, we will see the Princess first. Michel, could you ask her to come in?'

Princess Dragomiroff looked even uglier than the day before, but intelligence and energy shone from her small, dark eyes.

As M. Bouc apologised for troubling her, she stopped him in her deep, clear voice. 'Murder is a serious matter, Monsieur. I am happy to help you in any way that I can.'

'Thank you, Madame,' said Poirot. 'You are Princess Natalia Dragomiroff, travelling to your home in Paris?'

'Yes. My maid is with me.'

'Please could you tell us your movements last night after dinner?'

'Willingly. I went to bed straight after the meal. I read until eleven, then turned out the light. I was unable to sleep because of pains that I often have in my legs. At about a quarter to one I rang for my maid. She read to me until I felt sleepy. I am not sure exactly when she left me. After half an hour, perhaps.'

'You have been in America, I suppose, Madame?'

The sudden change of subject surprised the old lady.

'Many times.'

'Did you at any time meet a family called Armstrong?'

Her voice shook as she said, 'If you mean Sonia and Robert Armstrong, then yes. Sonia was my goddaughter. Her mother, the actress Linda Arden, was a close friend of mine.'

'Linda Arden is dead now?'

'She is alive, but she sees no one. Her health is very poor.'

'There was, I think, a second daughter?'

'Yes, much younger than Mrs Armstrong.'

'Where is she now?'

The old woman looked at him in surprise. 'What connection do these questions have with the murder on this train?'

'The murdered man was responsible for the kidnap and murder of Mrs Armstrong's child.'

'Ah!' Princess Dragomiroff sat straighter in her chair. 'Then this murder is a very happy event. You will excuse my strong opinion on the subject.'

'Of course, Madame. Now we must return to my earlier question. Where is the younger daughter of Linda Arden?'

'I honestly cannot tell you, Monsieur. I have lost contact with her. I believe she married an Englishman some years ago, but I'm afraid I cannot remember his name.' She paused for a minute and then said, 'Is there anything else, gentlemen?'

'Just one thing, Madame. The colour of your dressing gown.'

'I suppose you have a good reason for asking this. It is blue.'

'That is all. Thank you for your help.'

Count and Countess Andrenyi were called next, but the Count entered the restaurant carriage alone.

He was a fine-looking man – tall, well-built, with a long moustache and dressed in an expensive English suit.

'Well, gentlemen,' he said, 'what can I do for you?'

'As you know,' said Poirot, 'there was a murder here last night, and I must ask certain questions of the passengers.'

'Of course. I am afraid, though, that my wife and I were asleep and heard nothing at all.'

'Do you know who was murdered, Monsieur?'

'The big American, I understand.'

'Yes. His name was Cassetti. He was responsible for some terrible crimes in America.'

The Count showed no sign of emotion at this news. 'That explains his murder, I suppose,' he said.

'You have been to America perhaps, Monsieur?'

'I was in Washington for a year.'

'Did you know the Armstrong family?'

'Armstrong – Armstrong – it is difficult to remember. There were so many names.' He smiled. 'But returning to the murder, gentleman, what more can I do to help you?'

'When did you go to bed last night, Monsieur?'

'At about eleven o'clock. We both slept until morning and noticed nothing. I am sorry we cannot help you in any way.'

'Thank you, Monsieur.'

'You won't need to speak to my wife. She can tell you nothing more than I have.'

Poirot's expression changed slightly. 'I am sure that is true,' he said. 'But I must have a little talk with the Countess.'

'It is quite unnecessary,' said the Count.

'I'm afraid it *is* necessary – for my report, you understand.'

'As you wish,' he said, and went to tell her.

Poirot looked at the Count's passport. *Travelling with wife*, he read.

Name: Elena Maria Andrenyi
Surname before marriage: Goldenberg
Age: 20

An ink spot had been dropped on the page by a careless official.

Countess Andrenyi entered the restaurant carriage. 'You wish to see me, gentlemen?' she asked in perfect French.

'Thank you, Countess,' said Poirot. 'I only need to ask you if you saw or heard anything unusual last night.'

'No, nothing. I had taken medicine to help me sleep.'

'Did you go with your husband to America, Madame?'

'Why did you ask me that?'

'No, Monsieur. We were not married then. We have only been married a year.' She smiled shyly. With her big, dark eyes and bright red lips, she looked very foreign – and very beautiful. 'Why did you ask me that?'

'Detectives have to ask a lot of strange questions. For example, what colour is your dressing gown?'

'It is a cream colour. Is that important?'

'Very important. And does your husband smoke a pipe?'

'No – cigarettes, but not a pipe.'

'Do you speak English?' he asked in that language.

'I speak a little, yes.' Her accent was strong, but very attractive.

'And that is all,' the detective said. 'You see, Madame, it was not so terrible.'

She smiled and walked out of the carriage.

'That was not very useful,' said M. Bouc. 'Shall we see the Italian now?'

Poirot did not reply for a moment. He was studying the ink spot on the Hungarian passport. Finally he looked at M. Bouc. 'We will leave your Italian for the moment, my friend, and interview the good-looking Englishman, Colonel Arbuthnot.'

When the Colonel arrived, Poirot said, 'You are travelling from India to Britain, I think. Why are you not going by boat?'

'I chose to take the overland route for reasons of my own,' said the Colonel unhelpfully.

'I see. You came straight through from India?'

'I stopped for three days in Baghdad to visit an old friend.'

'You met the young English lady there, perhaps – Miss Debenham?'

'No, I did not. I first met Miss Debenham on the train.'

'We think that M. Ratchett was murdered at a quarter past one last night. What were you doing at that time?'

'I was talking to the young American – the dead man's secretary. We were in his compartment.'

'Did you know M. MacQueen before this journey?'

'No. We started talking yesterday and we enjoyed each other's company. I don't usually like Americans, but I like MacQueen. We had a long discussion about India, and America, and the world in general. I was quite surprised when I looked at my watch and found that it was a quarter to two.'

'That is the time that you stopped this conversation?'

'Yes.'

'What did you do then?'

'I walked back to my own compartment and went to bed.'

'Now, Colonel, I want you to think back to your conversation with M. MacQueen. You got out at Vincovci?'

'Yes, but only for about a minute. It was snowing very hard.'

'So you came back in. You sat down again. You smoked –

'I chose to take the overland route for reasons of my own,' said the Colonel unhelpfully.

perhaps a cigarette, perhaps a pipe –' He paused for a moment.

'A pipe for me. MacQueen smoked cigarettes.'

'The train started again. Did anyone pass the door after that?'

'I don't remember anyone except the conductor. Wait a minute – there was a woman too, I think. She was wearing something red.'

'Thank you. Have you ever been in America, Colonel?'

'Never. I have no interest in going there.'

'Did you ever know a Colonel Armstrong?'

'Armstrong – Armstrong – I've known two or three Armstrongs. Do you mean Selby Armstrong? Or Tommy?'

'I mean Colonel Robert Armstrong, who married an American and whose only child was kidnapped and killed.'

'Ah, I remember reading about that. But I didn't know him.'

'The murdered man was responsible for that kidnap.'

'Really? Then he deserved to die – although it's a pity that it wasn't done legally, through the courts, of course. You can't go around murdering people out of revenge, like Corsicans.'

Poirot looked at the Colonel thoughtfully. 'I have no more questions – unless you noticed anything unusual last night?'

Arbuthnot thought for a moment. 'No,' he said. 'Nothing. Unless –' He paused.

'Yes?' said the detective.

'Well, it's nothing really. But when I got back to my compartment, I noticed that the door of the end compartment –'

'Number 16?'

'Yes, the door to it was not quite closed. The man inside looked out in a secretive way, then quickly closed the door. It seemed a bit strange.'

'Yes,' said Poirot doubtfully.

When the soldier had left the carriage, Poirot stared into space for some time. Then he said, 'Colonel Arbuthnot smokes a pipe. In M. Ratchett's compartment I found a pipe cleaner.'

'You think —?' began M. Bouc.

'He was also in the same army as Colonel Armstrong. He said that he did not know him, but perhaps that was a lie.'

'So it is possible that —?'

Poirot shook his head angrily. 'No, it is impossible that this Englishman, who believes in law and order, could push a knife into his enemy twelve times.'

Chapter 5 The Man with a Woman's Voice

The detective's thoughts turned to the next interview. 'The American in compartment 16, I think.'

The American soon came in, wearing a brightly coloured suit and a pink shirt. He had a wide, friendly face.

'Good morning, gentlemen,' he said. 'What can I do for you?'

'You have heard of this murder, Mr – er – Hardman?'

'Yes.'

'We are interviewing all the passengers. You are —' Poirot looked quickly at the passport in front of him. '— forty-one years of age, and a salesman of office machines?'

'Yes, that's me.'

'You are travelling for business reasons?'

'That's right.'

'Can you tell us anything about the events of last night?'

'Nothing at all. Sorry.'

'Ah, that is a pity. Perhaps, Mr Hardman, you will tell us exactly what you did after dinner last night?'

Hardman paused, then said, 'Excuse me, but who are you exactly?'

'I am Hercule Poirot. I have been hired by the Compagnie Internationale des Wagons Lits to solve this crime.'

'I've heard of you,' said Mr Hardman. He thought for a

minute more, then said, 'I suppose I should be honest.'

'You should certainly tell us all that you know,' said Poirot.

The American now spoke in a different voice – in fact, he seemed a completely different person. 'Well, as I said, I don't know anything. But I *should* know something.'

'Please explain, Mr Hardman.'

'Some of the information in my passport is false. This is who I really am.' He produced a card from his pocket.

Mr CYRUS B. HARDMAN

McNeil's Private Detectives

New York

Poirot knew the name of the company. McNeil's had an excellent reputation.

'I'd gone to Istanbul after a couple of criminals – no connection with this business. I was planning my journey home to New York when I got this.' He pushed across a letter.

Dear Sir,

I understand that you are a private detective. Please come to my rooms at four o'clock this afternoon.

It was written on notepaper from the Tokatlian Hotel in Istanbul and was signed 'S.E. Ratchett'.

'I went to see Ratchett, and he showed me some threatening letters that he had received. He hired me for protection on his journey west. Well, my protection wasn't very good, was it?'

'How had you hoped to protect him?'

'I had planned to travel in the next-door compartment, but it was taken. Number 16 was in a good position, though. No one could reach Mr Ratchett's compartment without passing mine.'

'You had no idea, I suppose, who the possible attacker was?'

'Well, I knew what he looked like. Mr Ratchett described him to me.'

'What?' His three listeners almost jumped out of their seats.

Hardman continued. 'A small man, dark, with a high voice

38

like a woman's. That's how Ratchett described him.'

'Did you know that Ratchett was Cassetti, the Armstrong murderer?' *a protector of Ratchett*

Mr Hardman looked shocked. 'No, I didn't recognise him. I'd seen photos of Cassetti in the papers, I suppose, but I wouldn't recognise my own mother in one of those photos.'

'Please, M. Hardman, continue your story.'

'There's not much to tell. I slept in the day and stayed awake watching the corridor at night. Nothing happened the first night and I thought the same was true last night. No stranger passed.'

'You are sure of that, M. Hardman?'

'Yes, I am. I'm certain.'

'Then I think we have finished. Thank you.' Poirot offered the American a cigarette. 'But perhaps you prefer a pipe?'

'Not me. It was nice to meet you, Mr Poirot.' He took a cigarette and walked away.

The three men looked at each other.

'A small man, dark, with a high voice like a woman's,' said M. Bouc thoughtfully.

'A description which fits no one on the train,' said Poirot. He paused, then said with a smile, 'And now we will make M. Bouc happy. We will see the Italian.'

A man with dark skin and a pleasant, cheerful face was soon walking across the restaurant carriage towards them.

'Your name is Antonio Foscarelli, from Italy?'

'Yes, Monsieur, but I have become an American citizen. It is better for my business.' He smiled.

'You sell Ford motor cars?'

'Yes, you see –'

A long explanation of Foscarelli's business methods followed, before Poirot could continue his questions. 'So you have lived in the United States for the last ten years?'

'Yes, Monsieur. I remember the day that I left. My mother –'

Poirot interrupted him. 'Did you ever meet Mr Ratchett in America?'

'No, but I met many people like him. On the outside, very polite, very well-dressed, but underneath – evil. In my opinion, Ratchett was a criminal.'

'Your opinion is correct,' said Poirot. 'Ratchett was Cassetti, the kidnapper.'

'What did I tell you? I am good at reading people's faces. It is important in my work.'

'You remember the Armstrong case?'

'Not very well. It was a little girl, wasn't it? A terrible crime, but these things happen, even in a great country like America.'

'Did you ever meet any members of the Armstrong family?'

'I don't think so, but it is difficult to say. Last year alone I sold cars to –'

Poirot interrupted him again. 'Monsieur, please tell me what you did last night after dinner.'

'With pleasure. I went back to my compartment. An English servant shares the compartment with me but he was out. Then he came back, but he wasn't interested in talking. "Yes", "No" – nothing else. He was very unfriendly. He read his book and I read mine. I smoked a cigarette or two. He had toothache, and he was making a lot of noise about it. I went to sleep, but I woke up a few times to the sound of his complaining.'

'Did he leave the compartment at all during the night?'

'I don't think so. When the door opens, the light from the corridor comes in very brightly and wakes you up.'

With words of thanks, Poirot brought the interview to an end.

'Well, he has been in America for a long time,' said M. Bouc when Foscarelli had left the carriage. 'He is Italian – Italians are good at lying and love using knives. I don't like Italians.'

'That is very clear,' smiled Poirot. 'But there is no evidence against this man. Italians use knives, yes, but in a fight, when

40

they are angry. This murder was very carefully planned.'

He picked up the last two passports. 'Let us see Miss Mary Debenham next.'

Miss Debenham entered the restaurant carriage calmly, dressed in a little black suit. She sat down opposite Poirot.

'Your name is Mary Hermione Debenham, you are English, and you are twenty-six years old?' began Poirot.

'Yes.'

'Now, Miss Debenham, what can you tell us about last night's events?'

'Nothing, I'm afraid. I went to bed and slept.'

Poirot looked at her thoughtfully. 'You are travelling from Baghdad to London, I believe.'

'Yes.'

'What have you been doing in Baghdad?'

'I have been working as governess to two children.'

'Have you ever been to America?'

'America? No, never.'

'What is your opinion of the lady who shares your compartment – Miss Ohlsson?'

'She seems a pleasant, simple person.'

'What colour is her dressing gown?'

Mary Debenham looked surprised. 'A brown colour.'

'And I noticed your dressing gown on the train to Istanbul. It is purple, I believe.'

'Yes, that is right.'

'Have you got any other dressing gown, Miss Debenham? A red one, for example?'

'No, that is not mine.'

The detective moved forward quickly, like a cat jumping on a mouse.

'Not yours? So you know that the red dressing gown belongs to someone else! Whose is it?'

41

The girl moved back, a little shocked. 'I don't know,' she replied. 'I saw someone wearing it last night in the corridor, but I didn't see her face.'

'Was she tall or short? Fair or dark?'

'She had a hat on, so I couldn't see her hair. But she was tall and thin. It was a Chinese-style dressing gown.'

'Yes, that's right, Chinese.' The detective was silent for a minute. Then he said to himself, 'I cannot understand. None of this makes sense.' Looking up, he said to Miss Debenham, 'We do not need you any more. You can go.'

When she had left, M. Bouc stared at his friend with a confused look on his face. 'You think she is guilty, don't you?' he said slowly. 'But why? She seems a very pleasant young lady – the last person in the world to be a murderer.'

'I agree,' said Constantine. 'She is a very calm person. She would not murder her enemy. She would take him to court.'

The girl moved back, a little shocked.

'There is an unemotional, intelligent brain behind this crime. Miss Debenham fits the description of the murderer exactly.'

M. Bouc shook his head. 'You are wrong, my friend. That young woman is not a criminal.'

'I have another reason to think carefully about her. I have not yet told you what I heard during my journey to Istanbul.'

He told the two men about Miss Debenham's words to Colonel Arbuthnot on the platform at Konya.

M. Bouc repeated the words thoughtfully. '"*Not now. When it's all over. When it's behind us.*" That is certainly strange. It suggests that she and the Colonel are both responsible.'

'Yes, but there are other people who tell us that they could not be the murderers. The stories of the Swedish woman and Mr MacQueen seem to prove that they are both innocent. No, that solution does not work. Ah well,' continued the detective, picking up the last passport, 'let us see our last passenger – Princess Dragomiroff's German maid, Hildegarde Schmidt.'

When the maid entered, Poirot asked her gently, in German, about her movements the night before.

'I do not know anything, Monsieur,' she said.

'Your employer sent for you last night, I believe. Do you remember the time?'

'No, Monsieur. I was asleep when the conductor called me.'

'Do you often go to your employer's room at night?'

'It is not unusual, Monsieur. She does not sleep well.'

'And did you put on your dressing gown to go to her compartment?'

'That would not be right, Monsieur! I put on my day clothes.'

'Although it is a very nice dressing gown – red, I think?'

She stared at him. 'It is dark blue, Monsieur!'

'Ah! My mistake! So, you went to the Princess's compartment. What did you do there?'

'I read to her. Then I returned to my own compartment to

get her an extra blanket, and finally went back to bed.'

'Do you know what time that was?'

'No, Monsieur.'

'And you met no one in the corridor?'

'No, Monsieur. There was nobody there except the conductor. Everyone was asleep.'

'But you did see the conductor. What was he doing?'

'He came out of one of the compartments, Monsieur.'

M. Bouc moved forward. 'Which one,' he asked urgently.

The maid looked frightened. 'One of the middle ones, Monsieur. Two or three doors from the Princess's.'

'Please tell us exactly what happened.'

'He almost ran into me as I was taking the blanket to the Princess. Then he apologised and continued down the corridor. A bell began ringing, but I do not think he answered it.'

'This poor conductor,' said Poirot. 'He had a busy night. First he had to wake you. Then there was that bell.'

'He was not the conductor who woke me, Monsieur. It was another one.'

'Another one? Would you recognise him if you saw him again?'

'I think so, Monsieur.'

Poirot whispered something in M. Bouc's ear. M. Bouc went to the door to give an order.

'Have you ever been to America?' the detective continued.

'Never, Monsieur. It must be a fine country.'

He took a handkerchief from his pocket. 'Is this yours?'

There was a moment's silence as the woman examined it. Her face went a little red. 'No, it is not mine,' she replied.

'It has the letter H, you see – for Hildegarde.'

'Really, it is not mine. This is an expensive handkerchief, Monsieur, the handkerchief of a fine lady.'

'You do not know *which* fine lady?'

Poirot noticed that there was a slight pause before she

answered, 'I? Oh, no, Monsieur.'

M. Bouc now whispered in Poirot's ear. The detective said, 'The three conductors are coming in, Mademoiselle. Please could you tell me which one almost ran into you last night?'

The three men entered. Hildegarde Schmidt looked at them and immediately shook her head.

'No, Monsieur. None of these is the man that I saw last night. These are all tall, big men. I saw a small, dark man with a little moustache. When he said "Excuse me", his voice was weak, like a woman's. I remember him very well, Monsieur.'

Chapter 6 The Sponge Bag

'A small dark man with a high voice,' said M. Bouc when the conductors and Hildegarde Schmidt had left the carriage. 'That is the enemy that Ratchett described! But where is he now? He didn't *leave* the train, but he isn't *on* the train either.'

'Like you, I am very confused,' said Poirot. 'In this situation, it is always best to return to the facts that we can be sure about.

'Fact one: Ratchett, or Cassetti, was murdered in his bed last night, with twelve knife wounds in the chest. Fact two: his watch had stopped at a quarter past one –'

'So that gives us a definite time for the crime,' said M. Bouc.

'Not necessarily,' said the detective. 'It is possible that the murder happened earlier or later than that time, and that the murderer has left us the watch as a false clue. There is also the information from Dr Constantine, that at least two of the wounds were made some time after Ratchett was already dead.'

'And what about the man in the conductor's uniform?' asked M. Bouc. 'He is fact three.'

'Not so fast, my friend. We must first examine the evidence carefully. Hardman, the detective, spoke of this man. Should we believe him? I think we should, because his story – that he was hired by Ratchett – could easily be disproved by a quick phone call to McNeil's in New York. And we have other evidence that his story is true, from Hildegarde Schmidt. Her description of the man in the conductor's uniform matches Hardman's description exactly. And there is also the button found in Mrs Hubbard's compartment. So we have three separate pieces of evidence for this man with the high voice.'

'Yes, yes, my friend,' said M. Bouc impatiently. 'We all agree that he exists. But where did he *go*?'

'Perhaps he is two people. I mean, he is both himself – the small, dark man feared by M. Ratchett – and a passenger on the train, looking so different that Ratchett did not recognise him.'

'But the men on the train are all tall,' said M. Bouc, '– except the servant Masterman, and he is unlikely to be our murderer.'

'The man may actually be a woman,' said Poirot. 'That would explain the high voice.'

'But it would not explain the wounds that did not bleed,' said Dr Constantine. 'We must not forget those.'

'I have forgotten nothing, Doctor, but I have not yet found the solution that I am looking for. Perhaps the woman in the red dressing gown, seen by several passengers including me, is our second murderer – the one who made those wounds, Doctor. If we believe the female passengers, nobody has a red dressing gown. So where is it now? And where is the conductor's uniform with the missing button?'

'Ah!' cried M. Bouc, jumping to his feet. 'We must search all the passengers' luggage.'

M. Poirot stood up too. 'I can guess where you will find the uniform,' he said. 'It will almost certainly be in the compartment of Hildegarde Schmidt.'

'How –' began M. Bouc, but he was interrupted by screams from the corridor. The door flew open and Mrs Hubbard ran in.

'It's too horrible!' she cried. 'In my sponge bag. My sponge bag! A great knife – with blood all over it.'

Then she suddenly fell forwards and dropped heavily into the arms of M. Bouc.

M. Bouc moved the woman to a chair, with her head on the table, and followed Poirot out of the door.

Dr Constantine called for a waiter. 'Keep her head like that,' he said, then hurried after the other two.

There was a crowd of people outside Mrs Hubbard's compartment, wanting to see what the screams were about.

Michel opened the door for the detective and his two friends.

'The knife is there, Monsieur. I have not touched it.'

Hanging on the handle of the door into the next compartment was a large sponge bag. Below it, on the floor, was a sharp knife, covered in dried blood. Poirot picked it up carefully.

'What do you think, Doctor? Did this knife kill Ratchett?'

Constantine's examination did not take long. 'Yes. All the wounds on Ratchett's body could be made with that knife.'

'So,' said M. Bouc, 'the man passes through this compartment on his way to the corridor. He notices the sponge bag and hides the knife inside it. Not even realising that he has woken Mrs Hubbard, he quickly leaves.'

'Yes, no doubt,' said Poirot, but his mind was clearly on other matters. He was staring at a door bolt thirty centimetres above the handle where the sponge bag was hanging.

His thoughts were interrupted by the tearful return of Mrs Hubbard. 'I'm not going to spend another night in this compartment,' she said. 'I wouldn't sleep in here again if you paid me a million dollars. Oh, if my daughter knew –'

Poirot said loudly, 'Your luggage will be moved immediately, Madame.'

Mrs Hubbard's crying stopped. 'Really?' she said. 'Then I feel better already.'

Poirot told Michel to move her luggage to compartment number 12, in the next carriage. The detective then showed her to her new compartment himself. She looked around happily.

'This is fine,' she said. 'And it faces the other way, so it feels quite different from my old compartment. Oh, I still can't believe that there was a murderer in there!'

'The bolt on the door still confuses me, Madame,' said Poirot. 'You were in bed, so you couldn't see it?'

'That's right, because the sponge bag was there.'

Poirot picked up the sponge bag and hung it on the door handle. 'I see,' he said. 'The bolt is just underneath the handle, so it is hidden by the sponge bag.'

'Exactly. But the Swedish lady said that it was bolted.'

'The Swedish lady said that it was bolted.'

'She made a mistake, I suppose,' said Poirot.

'Well, it was rather stupid of her, I think.'

Mrs Hubbard began to worry about the delay to the train. 'I can't possibly get to my boat in time. This is just too terrible –'

M. Poirot interrupted her before the tears returned. 'You have had a shock, Madame. Perhaps we should get you a cup of tea.'

'A coffee would be better. Thank you.'

As the coffee was brought to Mrs Hubbard, Poirot asked for permission to search her luggage. She agreed willingly, but nothing of interest was found. A search of Mr Hardman's compartment was no more successful, but in Colonel Arbuthnot's luggage he discovered a packet of pipe cleaners that were exactly the same as the one found at the crime scene.

Poirot went next to the compartments of Count and Countess Andrenyi. As he entered, the Count was sitting near the door, reading a newspaper. His wife was curled up in a chair near the window. It appeared that she had been asleep.

A quick search followed. 'Here is a label all wet on your suitcase, Madame,' said Poirot as he lifted down a blue bag.

She did not reply, but stayed curled on her chair, showing no interest in the visitors.

The next compartment was shared by Mary Debenham and Greta Ohlsson. Poirot explained his purpose. 'After we have examined your luggage, Miss Ohlsson, perhaps you could visit Mrs Hubbard. We have moved her into the next carriage, but she is still very upset. It might help her to talk to someone.'

The kind Swede wanted to go and see Mrs Hubbard immediately. She left her suitcase unlocked in the compartment for Poirot's search. This was quickly done and the detective turned to Miss Debenham. She was staring at him.

'Why did you send Miss Ohlsson away?' she asked him.

'To help the American woman,' he replied.

'A good excuse – but still an excuse.' She smiled. 'You wanted to speak to me alone, didn't you?'

'I do not plan as carefully as you think, Miss Debenham.'

'Please – I am not stupid. For some reason, you have decided that I am responsible for this horrible crime.'

'You are imagining things.'

'No, I am not imagining things. Let's not waste time. Say what you want to say.'

'As you wish, Mademoiselle. On the journey from Syria, we stopped at Konya and I went for a walk on the platform. I heard you say to Colonel Arbuthnot, "Not now. When it's all over. When it's behind us." What did you mean by those words?'

She said very quietly, 'Do you think I meant – murder?'

'I am asking you what you meant.'

She sat silently for a minute, lost in thought. Then she said, 'Those words had a meaning that I cannot tell you, Monsieur. I can only promise you that I never saw this man Ratchett in my life until I saw him on this train.'

'You refuse to explain those words?'

'I must, I'm afraid. There was something that I had to do –'

'And now you have done it?'

'What do you mean?'

'There was a delay before we arrived in Istanbul. You were very upset – you, who are always so calm. You lost that calm.'

'I did not want to miss my connection.'

'But the Orient Express leaves Istanbul every day of the week. Missing the connection meant a delay of only twenty-four hours. On this train, again we have had a delay – a more serious delay. But this time your behaviour is very different. You are not impatient at all. You are quite calm.'

Miss Debenham's face was red. She was not smiling now.

'You do not answer, Mademoiselle?'

'I'm sorry. What do you want me to tell you?' For the first time she showed signs of losing her temper.

50

'Tell me why your behaviour is so different.'

'I cannot tell you. There is nothing to explain.'

'It does not matter,' said Hercule Poirot. 'I will find out.' He turned and left the compartment.

In the next compartment, Hildegarde Schmidt was waiting for them. After looking through her luggage, Poirot turned to M. Bouc. 'You remember what I said? Look here a moment.'

There was a brown conductor's uniform untidily placed inside the maid's suitcase.

The maid suddenly looked frightened. 'That is not mine!' she cried. 'I have not looked in that case since we left Istanbul.'

Poirot touched her arm gently and said, 'Do not worry. We believe you. The man in this uniform had hoped not to be seen. After he ran into you in the corridor, he needed to hide his uniform. He saw that the door to your compartment was open, so he quickly took it off and threw it on top of your suitcase.'

He held up the jacket. A button, the third down, was missing. In the pocket was a conductor's key.

'With that, he could lock and unlock any door in the carriage,' cried M. Bouc.

'Now we must find the red dressing gown,' said Poirot.

The next compartment was Mr MacQueen's, and after that Masterman's and the Italian's. Nothing of interest was found in their luggage, and there were no more compartments to search.

'What shall we do now?' asked M. Bouc.

'We have collected all the evidence that we can. We will go now to the restaurant carriage and think. But I will need cigarettes. I will meet you there in a few moments.'

Poirot returned to his own compartment to get cigarettes from his suitcase. As he opened the case, he sat down suddenly and stared. Placed tidily among his things was a red dressing gown with a Chinese picture on the back.

Chapter 7 Which of Them?

M. Bouc and Dr Constantine were talking together when Poirot entered the restaurant carriage.

'Well,' said M. Bouc, 'this case makes no sense at all.'

'I agree,' said the doctor.

Poirot lit a cigarette. 'But the evidence of the passengers was very helpful.'

'I thought it told us nothing!' cried Bouc. 'What did I miss?'

'Take young MacQueen, for example. He told us that his employer, M. Ratchett, spoke no languages except English. Last night the conductor heard someone in M. Ratchett's compartment call out, "*Ce n'est rien. Je me suis trompé.*" That was not M. Ratchett.'

'It is true!' cried Constantine excitedly. 'That is why you didn't want to accept the evidence of the watch. Those words came from the compartment at twenty-three minutes to one. Ratchett was already dead –'

'And it was his murderer speaking,' finished M. Bouc.

'You go too fast, my friends,' said Poirot. 'We have no evidence that Ratchett was dead at that time.'

'There was the cry that woke you.'

'Yes, that is true.'

'In one way,' said M. Bouc, 'this discovery does not change things very much. The murderer killed Ratchett half an hour earlier than we first thought. He stayed in the compartment for half an hour, changed the watch hands to a quarter past one and left through Mrs Hubbard's compartment.'

'But imagine that you are the murderer,' said Poirot. 'Wouldn't you change the watch to a time when your presence in Ratchett's compartment was impossible? You wouldn't move the hands to the exact time that you left the crime scene.'

'True,' said Dr Constantine, a little confused.

'Perhaps it was the second murderer who changed the watch,' said M. Bouc. 'The woman in the red dressing gown.'

'It was too dark for her to see that the man was already dead, but she managed to find a watch in Ratchett's pyjama pocket and change the time blindly!' said Poirot in disbelief.

M. Bouc gave him a cold stare. 'And what is your explanation, my friend?'

'At the moment I have none that makes sense,' replied Poirot. 'But it is time to close our eyes and think. One or more of the passengers killed Ratchett. Which of them?'

For a quarter of an hour, no one spoke. Poirot appeared to be asleep. Then suddenly his eyes opened and he said to himself, 'But why not? If so – well, that would explain everything.'

He turned to the other men in the carriage and asked, 'Have you had any useful thoughts?'

'Thoughts, yes, but nothing very useful,' said the doctor.

M. Bouc agreed.

'I myself have thought of an explanation that would cover all the facts of the case. I am not yet sure that it is the correct one, but I will soon find out. Before that, let us discuss some points of interest. Firstly, an ink spot on a Hungarian passport.'

M. Bouc looked at the passport of Count and Countess Andrenyi. 'Is this the spot that you mean?' he asked.

'Yes. It seems to be fresh ink. You notice where it is?'

'At the beginning of the Countess's name. But what –?'

'Now, let us think back to the handkerchief. It is a very expensive thing, hand-made in Paris. It has an H on it, but it is not something that unfashionable Mrs Hubbard would buy, and it is certainly not the handkerchief of Hildegarde, the lady's maid. There are only two women on the train who might own a handkerchief like this. They are Princess Dragomiroff –'

'Whose first name is Natalia,' interrupted M. Bouc.

'– and Countess Andrenyi. Now, I wonder about that ink

spot. Perhaps it was just an accident, but perhaps it is hiding a letter. Perhaps the Countess's name is not Elena but Helena.'

'Helena!' cried M. Bouc. 'That is an idea.'

'And there is something to support that idea too. One of the labels on the Countess's luggage was slightly wet. Perhaps there too a change to her name was made.'

'I am starting to believe you,' said M. Bouc. 'But the Countess Andrenyi, a murderer? It is so unlikely.'

'Now, let us imagine last night without the snow on the line. What happens? Well, the murder is discovered as the train enters Italy. The man in conductor's uniform is seen earlier – just before one o'clock. We find a button in Mrs Hubbard's compartment and the uniform in the toilets. We read the threatening letters produced by MacQueen. We decide that the murderer got off the train at Brod, where it stopped at 00.58.'

'You mean –?'

'I mean that the murder was planned to seem like the work of someone from the outside, not a passenger. But the snow changed everything. It made it impossible to believe that the murderer had got off the train.'

'And where does the handkerchief fit in?'

'Be patient, my friend. Now, we return to the burnt note which included the words *Daisy Armstrong*. The murderer did not want us to read that letter. Why not? There can be only one reason. Someone on this train must be very closely connected to the Armstrong family, and the note would make that person look guilty. I think that person is Countess Andrenyi.'

'But what connection could she have with the Armstrongs?' cried M. Bouc. 'She says that she has never been to America.'

'Yes, and she speaks only a little English, and she has a very foreign appearance. But this could all be an act. I am guessing that she is Linda Arden's younger daughter. Arden was not the actress's real surname. Perhaps she was really called Goldenberg, and the daughter met and married Count Andrenyi while he was working in Washington.'

'But the Princess says that she married an Englishman.'

'Princess Dragomiroff says that she cannot remember the name of the daughter's husband. Is that likely, when the Princess and the actress were such close friends?'

One of the waiters interrupted them. 'Excuse me, Monsieur Bouc, but should we serve dinner now?'

M. Bouc looked at Poirot.

'I think dinner would be most welcome,' said the detective.

At dinner, Poirot shared a table with M. Bouc and the doctor.

The other passengers spoke little – even Mrs Hubbard. Poirot heard her say, 'I don't think I can eat,' then watched as she ate everything that was offered to her.

Poirot had asked the waiter to serve the Count and Countess Andrenyi last. All the other tables were empty when they finished their meal. As they stood up, Poirot stepped towards them. 'You have dropped your handkerchief, Madame,' he said, passing the Countess the small square of material.

She looked at it quickly, then gave it back to him. 'You are mistaken, Monsieur. That is not my handkerchief.'

'But it has a letter H on it – the first letter of your name.'

She said calmly, 'My name is Elena. The first letter is E.'

'I think not,' said Poirot. 'Your name is Helena, not Elena. You are Helena Goldenberg, the sister of Mrs Armstrong.'

There was complete silence for a minute or two. Both the Count and the Countess had gone white. Poirot said, more gently, 'You cannot deny it. We know.'

'It is true, Monsieur,' said the Countess. Her voice had changed. It was, for the first time, American.

'Why did you not tell me that this morning, Madame? And why did you change the name on your passport?'

'*I* changed the name – it was not my wife,' said the Count. 'We had heard that a handkerchief with an H on it had been discovered by the murdered man's body.'

Helena spoke in an emotional voice. 'The dead man murdered my niece, killed my sister and caused the death of my sister's husband – the three people that I loved best in all the world. I had such a good reason for killing him.'

'And did you kill him, Madame?'

'I promise you that I did not.' she said quietly.

'It is true,' said the Count. 'Helena never left her compartment last night.' He paused, then continued, 'Imagine my position, M. Poirot. I did not want my wife, who I knew was innocent, to be taken to a police station, questioned, perhaps even judged guilty and sent to prison.'

'If I am going to believe you, you must help me,' said Poirot.

'Help you?' repeated the Countess.

'*I had such a good reason for killing him.*'

'Yes. The reason for the murder lies in the past – in the deaths of your sister and her family. Take me back into the past so that I can find the connection that explains everything.'

'What can I tell you? They are all dead. All dead – Robert, Sonia, dear little Daisy.'

'Susanne too. What nationality was she, Madame?'

'Poor Susanne. She was French.'

'Her surname?'

'It's terrible, but I can't remember – we all just called her Susanne. A pretty, cheerful girl. She was so fond of Daisy. She helped the nurse to look after her.'

'Who was the nurse?'

'Stengelberg was her name. She too loved Daisy.'

'You yourself – you were a young girl at the time – did you have a governess?'

'Oh, yes, a very frightening woman. She was English – no, Scottish – a big, red-haired lady in her forties.'

'What was her name?'

'Miss Freebody.'

'And there was no one else living with you?'

'Only servants.'

'Now, Madame, I want you to think carefully before you answer this question. Have you, since you were on this train, seen anyone that you recognised?'

She stared at him. 'I? No, no one.'

'What about Princess Dragomiroff?'

'Oh, I know her, of course. I thought you meant anyone – anyone from – from that time.'

'I did, Madame. Some years have passed, remember. The person may look very different now.'

She thought for a moment. 'No – I am sure – there is no one.'

When the Count and Countess had left the carriage, M. Bouc cried, 'Excellent work, my friend. I never for one moment imagined that the Countess could be our murderer.'

'So you feel sure that she is guilty?' asked M. Poirot.

'Yes. The handkerchief proves it,' said M. Bouc confidently.

'Oh, I am not sure about the handkerchief. There is another person who could be its owner, remember. I –'

He stopped suddenly as Princess Dragomiroff entered the restaurant carriage. She walked towards Poirot and said, 'I believe, Monsieur, that you have a handkerchief of mine.'

'Is this it, Madame?' He showed her the one found in Ratchett's compartment.

'That is it. It has a letter N in the corner, for my name Natalia.'

'But, Madame, it has the letter H, not N,' said M. Bouc.

She gave him a cold stare. 'My handkerchiefs always have Russian letters on them. H is N in Russian.'

There was something about this old lady that made M. Bouc feel very foolish.

'You did not tell us that this handkerchief was yours when we questioned you this morning,' he said.

'You did not ask me,' said the Princess. 'Your next question, I suppose, will be – why was my handkerchief lying by a murdered man's body? My reply to that is that I have no idea.'

'Please excuse me, Madame, but why would we believe you?' said Poirot. 'You have already lied to us about Mrs Armstrong's younger sister.'

'And I would do the same again. Her mother was my friend. I believe in loyalty – to friends, to family – above all else.'

'And in the case of the handkerchief, perhaps you are again lying to protect your friend's daughter.'

'You think that the handkerchief is Helena's?' She smiled coldly. 'Well, it is easy to prove that it is mine. I will give you the address of the people in Paris who made it for me.'

'Your maid, Madame, did she recognise this handkerchief when we showed it to her this morning?'

'Probably. She saw it and said nothing? Ah, well, then she too can be loyal.'

She stood up and walked out of the restaurant carriage.

'But the Princess cannot be our murderer,' said Dr Constantine. 'She doesn't have the strength to make the deepest wounds. Her arms are very weak.'

'But the smaller wounds?'

'Yes, those could be her work, I suppose.'

M. Bouc shook his head. 'Lies – and more lies. I cannot believe how many lies we were told this morning!'

'There are many more lies to uncover,' said Poirot cheerfully. 'I just need to make some more lucky guesses.'

Chapter 8 Two Solutions

Colonel Arbuthnot was called again to the restaurant carriage. He came in, clearly annoyed, and said, 'Well?'

'Firstly, I would like to show you a pipe cleaner.' Poirot held it up. 'Is it one of yours?'

'I don't know. I don't put a private mark on them!'

'You are the only passenger who smokes a pipe. This pipe cleaner was found by the body of the murdered man. Can you tell us, Colonel, how it got there?'

Colonel Arbuthnot looked surprised. 'I don't know,' he said. 'I can only tell you that I didn't drop it there myself.'

'Did you murder Mr Ratchett?'

'I never even spoke to the man. Although, if I was the murderer, I wouldn't tell you, would I?'

'Oh well. It doesn't matter.' Again, the Colonel looked surprised. 'I really wanted to see you about something else,' continued Poirot. 'Miss Debenham has told you that I heard her talking to you on the platform at Konya?'

Arbuthnot did not reply.

'She said, "*Not now. When it's all over. When it's behind us.*" Do you know what those words meant?'

'I must refuse to answer that question.'

'You will not tell a lady's secrets?'

'Exactly.'

'Even when that lady is likely to be guilty of murder?'

'That is crazy. Miss Debenham is not a murderer.'

'Miss Debenham was the Armstrongs' governess at the time that Daisy was kidnapped,' said Poirot.

There was a minute's silence.

'You see, we know more than you think,' continued Poirot. 'If Miss Debenham is innocent, why did she say that she had never been to America?'

The Colonel coughed. 'Perhaps you are mistaken.'

'No, I am not mistaken. Why did Miss Debenham lie to me?'

'I suggest that you ask *her*. I still think that you are wrong.'

Poirot called to one of the waiters. 'Go and ask the English lady in number 11 to come here, please.'

The four men sat in silence until Miss Debenham had entered the carriage. Her head was thrown back bravely. She looked very beautiful.

Her eyes went to Arbuthnot for a moment – just a moment. Then she said to Poirot, 'You wished to see me?'

'I wished to ask you, Mademoiselle, why you told us that you had never been in America. We now know that you were living in the Armstrongs' house when Daisy was kidnapped.'

Her face changed for a second, then returned to its usual calm. 'The reason for my lie is easy to explain,' she said with a smile. 'I have to work. Do you know how hard it is to get and keep a good job as a governess? If my name were connected with this crime, if my photograph were in the English newspapers, my reputation would be ruined. I would never work again.'

'But if you were not guilty, there would be no problem.'

'People remember names and faces – they do not remember who was guilty and who was innocent.'

'It is always better to be honest, Mademoiselle. And you also kept secret the fact that Countess Andrenyi is Mrs Armstrong's younger sister.'

'Countess Andrenyi? Really?' She shook her head. 'It may seem unlikely, but I honestly didn't recognise her. Three years ago, when I last saw her, she was an American schoolgirl. She looks so different! It is true that, when I saw her, her face looked familiar. But I couldn't think who she was. After that, I didn't really notice her. I had my own worries.'

'You will not tell me your secret?' asked Poirot gently.

She replied very quietly, 'I can't – I can't.' Suddenly her face was in her hands and she was crying. She seemed heartbroken.

The Colonel jumped up and stood uncomfortably beside her. He shouted at Poirot, 'I'll break every bone in your body!'

'Monsieur!' cried M. Bouc.

Arbuthnot was now talking to the girl. 'Mary, please –'

She jumped up. 'It's nothing,' she said. 'I'm fine. You don't need me any more, do you, M. Poirot? If you do, please come and find me. Oh, what a fool I'm making of myself!'

She hurried out of the carriage, followed by Arbuthnot.

'Well, my friend,' smiled M. Bouc at Poirot, 'another excellent guess!'

'How do you do it?' asked Dr Constantine in admiration.

'This time it was easy. Countess Andrenyi almost told me.'

'What?!'

'When I asked her governess's name, she said Freebody. You may not know, gentlemen, but there used to be a shop in London called Debenham and Freebody. With the name Debenham running through her head, Freebody was the first name that the Countess could think of. I understood immediately, of course.'

'Nothing would surprise me now,' said M. Bouc. 'Even if everybody on the train proved to be friends of the Armstrongs!'

'It is certainly a *most* surprising case,' said Dr Constantine.

'Now, let us see your Italian, M. Bouc,' said Poirot. He asked the waiter to call Foscarelli to the restaurant carriage.

The big Italian soon arrived, looking very nervous. 'What do you want?' he said. 'I have told you everything that I know.'

'But now we want the true story,' said Poirot. 'We already know it, but it will be better for you if you tell us yourself.'

'You sound like the American police,' he said angrily. ' "Be honest with us," they say, "and the judges will be kind to you." '

'Ah! You have had experience of the New York police?'

'No, no, never. They could not prove anything against me – although they tried hard enough.'

'That was in the Armstrong case, wasn't it?' said Poirot quietly. 'You drove their cars for them?' His eyes met the Italian's.

'If you already know, why ask me?' the Italian said.

'Why did you lie this morning?'

'For business reasons, and because I do not want to be questioned by the Yugoslav police. They hate Italians. They would just throw me in prison.'

'Perhaps you deserve to be thrown in prison.'

'No, no, I didn't murder that man. The long-faced Englishman can tell you that.'

'Very good,' said Poirot. 'You can go.'

'That man was a pig!' cried Foscarelli as he left the carriage. There were tears in his eyes. 'Little Daisy – what a lovely child! She loved to play in my car. All the servants thought she was wonderful.'

Next Poirot called Greta Ohlsson. She soon arrived, in tears, and fell back into the seat facing the detective.

'Do not upset yourself, Mademoiselle,' Poirot said gently. 'You were the nurse who looked after little Daisy Armstrong?'

'It is true,' cried the unhappy woman. 'Ah, she was a sweet, kind-hearted little girl.' For a moment she could not continue. 'I was wrong not to tell you this morning, but I was afraid – afraid. I was so happy that the evil man was dead, that he could not kill any more little children.'

Poirot touched her gently on the shoulder. 'I understand – I understand everything. I will ask you no more questions.'

The Swedish lady moved slowly out of the carriage, her eyes blind with tears. As she reached the door, she walked into a man coming in. It was the manservant, Masterman.

'Excuse me, sir,' he said to Poirot in his usual, unemotional voice. 'I thought I should tell you immediately. I worked for Colonel Armstrong in the war, sir, and afterwards in New York. I'm sorry that I didn't tell you earlier.'

He stopped.

Poirot stared at him. 'Is that all that you want to say?'

'Yes, sir.' He paused; then, when Poirot did not speak, he turned and left the carriage.

'This is more unlikely than a murder mystery novel!' cried Dr Constantine.

M. Bouc agreed. 'Of the twelve passengers, nine have got a definite connection with the Armstrong case.'

'Perhaps we can fit them *all* into our little collection,' said Poirot, smiling. 'Maybe they are – I don't know – the Armstrongs' gardener, housekeeper and cook.'

'That would be too much to believe,' said M. Bouc. 'They cannot all be connected.'

Poirot looked at him. 'You do not understand,' he said. 'You do not understand at all.'

'Do you?' asked M. Bouc. 'Do you know who killed Ratchett?'

'Oh, yes,' Poirot said. 'I have known for some time.'

Poirot was silent for a minute. Then he said, 'M. Bouc, could you please call everyone here. There are two possible solutions to this case. I want to explain them both to you all.'

The passengers crowded into the restaurant carriage and took their seats at the tables. They all looked nervous.

The conductor, Michel, asked M. Poirot if he could stay.

'Of course, Michel,' the detective replied.

He stood up and gave a little cough. 'Ladies and gentlemen, we are here to find out who murdered Samuel Edward Ratchett – also known as Cassetti. There are two possible solutions to the crime. I will explain both solutions, and ask M. Bouc and Dr Constantine here to judge which is the right one.

'Mr Ratchett died last night between midnight and two in the morning. At half an hour after midnight, the train stopped because of the thick snow. After that time it was impossible for anyone to leave the train.

'Here is my first solution. An enemy of Mr Ratchett got onto the train at Belgrade. He was wearing a conductor's uniform and had a conductor's key, with which he opened Ratchett's locked door. He attacked Ratchett with a knife and killed him. Then he went into Mrs Hubbard's compartment –'

'That's true,' said Mrs Hubbard.

'He put his knife in Mrs Hubbard's sponge bag. Without knowing it, he lost a button from his uniform. Then he went out into the corridor, threw his uniform into a suitcase in an empty compartment and, dressed in ordinary clothes, left the train at Vincovci through the door near the restaurant car.'

'But that explanation does not work!' cried M. Bouc. 'What about the voice heard inside his compartment at twenty-three minutes to one?'

'That was not Ratchett and not the murderer, but someone else. Perhaps someone had gone to speak to Ratchett and found him dead. He rang the bell to tell the conductor. Then, at the last minute, he changed his mind because he was afraid that people would think he was guilty of the crime.'

Princess Dragomiroff was looking at Poirot strangely. 'And the evidence of my maid, who saw the man in uniform at a quarter past one?' she asked. 'How do you explain that?'

'It is simple, Madame. She recognised your handkerchief and invented her story to protect you.'

'You have thought of everything,' said the Princess.

There was silence. Then everyone jumped as Dr Constantine suddenly hit the table with his hand. 'But no,' he said. 'No, no, and again no! That explanation does not work for so many reasons. You must know that perfectly well, Poirot.'

'Then I must give my second solution,' said the detective. 'But do not forget this first one too quickly. You may agree with it later.'

Poirot looked around the carriage before continuing, 'It was immediately clear to me that many of you were lying. To protect someone, Mr Hardman, you should spend the night in the person's compartment or in a place where you can see his door. Your method was completely useless – except for producing evidence that no one in any other part of the train could be Ratchett's murderer.

'Then there were Miss Debenham and Colonel Arbuthnot. On the platform at Konya, he called her Mary. A man like the Colonel does not use a woman's first name when he has only just met her. Clearly they were lying about their relationship.

'Mrs Hubbard also made a mistake. She said that her sponge bag was hanging on the handle of the door to Ratchett's compartment, and that it hid the bolt on the door. That would be possible in compartments 2, 4 and 12, for example – all the even numbers – because the bolt is just under the door handle. But in her compartment, number 3, the bolt is a long way *above* the handle and so it could not be hidden by a hanging sponge bag. Mrs Hubbard had clearly invented that story.

'The watch in Ratchett's pyjamas was interesting too. What an uncomfortable place to keep a watch! I was sure that it was a false clue. So was Ratchett murdered earlier, when a cry came from his room? I think not. He was so heavily drugged that he could not defend himself. He could not cry out either. I believe that the cry at twenty-three minutes to one – and the words in French – were planned to confuse me. MacQueen told me that Ratchett spoke no French. I was meant to think that Ratchett was killed at that moment.

'And the real time of the crime? I think Ratchett was killed at almost two o'clock. And the murderer?' He paused, looking at the passengers. There was complete silence.

He continued slowly. 'Everyone was proved innocent by another passenger – in most cases, a passenger who was unlikely to be a friend in an earlier life. MacQueen and Arbuthnot, the English manservant and the Italian, the Swedish lady and the English governess. "This is very strange," I said to myself. "They cannot all be guilty."

'And then, ladies and gentlemen, I realised. They *were* all guilty. It was impossible that so many people connected with the Armstrongs were travelling on the same train by chance. It could only happen if it was planned. That would also explain the crowded train at a time of year that is usually quiet. There were twelve passengers, after Ratchett's death. There were twelve knife wounds in Ratchett's body. In America, murder cases are decided by a group of twelve ordinary people.

'Ratchett had escaped punishment from the court in America, although no one doubted that he was guilty. I imagined a group of twelve people who decided, when the court case failed, to give him his punishment another way. And immediately the whole case became clear to me.

'Everything was explained – the strange wounds that did not bleed, the false threatening letters that were written only to be produced as evidence, the description of the dark man with a high voice that fitted none of the real conductors and could equally mean a man or a woman. I believe that everyone entered Ratchett's compartment through Mrs Hubbard's – and struck! No one could know which strike actually killed him.

'Every detail of the evidence was very carefully planned. The only possible solution appeared to be a murderer who joined the train and left again during the night. But then there was the snow – the first piece of bad luck. I imagine that there was a quick discussion, and everyone decided to continue with the crime. It would be clear that the murderer had to be one or more of the passengers, but they were still protected by each other's stories. They added some extra clues to confuse the case – a pipe cleaner, a lady's handkerchief, a woman in a red dressing gown. The dressing gown was probably Countess Andrenyi's, as there is no dressing gown in her luggage.

'MacQueen learnt that we had seen the word *Armstrong* on

He paused, looking at the passengers. There was complete silence.

the burnt letter, and told the others. It was their second piece of bad luck. The position of Countess Andrenyi became worrying, and the Count changed her name on the passport.

'The plan was impossible without the help of Michel, the conductor. But if he was one of the group, then there were thirteen people, not twelve. I believe that the Countess, who had the strongest reason to kill Cassetti, was probably the one who did not do it. Her husband has promised me that she did not leave her compartment. I believe him.

'But why was honest Michel in this? He was a good man who had worked on the train for many years. Then I remembered Susanne, the Armstrongs' French maid. Perhaps the unlucky girl was Michel's daughter. And the others? Arbuthnot was probably an army friend of Armstrong's, Hildegarde Schmidt the family's cook. Hardman probably worked as a detective on the case, or perhaps he had been in love with Susanne. And then there was Mrs Hubbard. She had a difficult job, because she was in the compartment through which everyone reached Ratchett. No one could say that they were with her. To play the part of this foolish old woman, a true actress was needed – Mrs Armstrong's mother, Linda Arden.'

He stopped.

Then, in a soft rich dreamy voice, very unlike the one she had used on the journey, Mrs Hubbard said, 'I always liked playing amusing characters. That mistake with the sponge bag was silly, though. We tried it on the journey east, but I was in an even numbered compartment then, I suppose.'

She moved slightly and looked straight at Poirot. 'You have guessed so much, M. Poirot. But even you can't imagine what it was like – that terrible day in New York when Hector MacQueen told us that Cassetti had walked free from the court. I was crazy with sadness and anger – and the servants were too. Colonel Arbuthnot was there. He was Robert Armstrong's best friend.'

'He saved my life in the war,' said Arbuthnot.

'We decided then and there to give him the punishment that the court had failed to give him – death. Perhaps we were mad – I don't know. There were twelve of us – well, eleven, because Susanne's father was in France, of course. Mary planned all the details with Hector.

'It took a long time to perfect our plan. Hardman managed to find Ratchett. Then Masterman and Hector had to get jobs with him. We had a meeting with Susanne's father. For Colonel Arbuthnot, it was important that there were twelve of us – it made it more correct, he thought. Michel was willing. We knew that Ratchett would come back from the East on the Orient Express, so this seemed the perfect opportunity.

'We tried to book every compartment in the carriage, but unfortunately one had been booked long before for someone from the train company.' She smiled at M. Bouc. 'Mr Harris, of course, was invented – we didn't want a stranger in Hector's compartment. Then, at the last minute, *you* came, M. Poirot.'

She stopped. 'Well,' she said, 'you know everything now. But what are you going to do about it? If someone must be punished, can't you blame me and *only* me for the crime? It's unnecessary to bring trouble to all these other good people – poor Michel – and Mary and Colonel Arbuthnot – they love each other so much –'

Poirot looked at his friend. 'What do you say, M. Bouc?'

M. Bouc coughed and said, 'In my opinion, the first solution was the correct one – definitely. The murderer left the train at Vincovci. I suggest that we give that solution to the Yugoslav police when they arrive. Do you agree, Doctor?'

'Certainly I agree,' said Dr Constantine. 'I think I made some – er – rather silly suggestions about the medical evidence.'

'Then,' said Poirot, 'we have solved the case. My work here is done.'

ACTIVITIES

Chapter 1

Before you read

1 You are going to read a story by Agatha Christie. She also wrote *Death on the Nile* and many other stories. Have you read or seen films of any of them? What do you know about them?

2 Look at the pictures in the book. When do you think the characters in the story lived?
  in the 1930s   in the 1960s   in the 1990s

3 Which three things will be important in the story? Use the title of the story and the Word List at the back of the book to help you guess.
  a forest   a ship   clues   evidence   a train   a wedding

4 Discuss these questions.
  a Have you ever spent the night in the sleeping compartment of a train? Describe the experience.
  b Would you like to have any of these people's jobs? What sort of work would you have to do?
    a lady's maid   a train conductor   a colonel
    a private detective   a governess   a diplomat
  c Have you got these things? What do you do with them?
    a sponge bag   aspirin   pyjamas

While you read

5 Match the people with the descriptions.
  a M. Poirot
  b Colonel Arbuthnot
  c Miss Debenham
  d M. Bouc
  e Mr MacQueen
  f Princess Dragomiroff
  g Mr Ratchett
  h Mrs Hubbard

  1) a young governess
  2) a rich but ugly old lady
  3) a man with cruel eyes
  4) a tall young American man
  5) a detective
  6) a middle-aged Englishman
  7) an old lady who talks a lot
  8) Poirot's friend, who works for a train company

70

After you read

6 Are these sentences true or false?

    a Colonel Arbuthnot and Miss Debenham do not seem to know each other very well. T

    b It is always difficult to get a sleeping compartment on the Orient Express. T

    c M. Poirot takes the bed of a man who booked but did not catch the train. T

    d Mr Ratchett thinks that someone wants to kill him. T

    e M. Poirot is going to try to protect Mr Ratchett. F

    f The train stops because a stranger is found in Mrs Hubbard's compartment. F

7 Discuss these questions.

    a Which character interests you most in this chapter? Why?

    b Would you like to travel on a train like the Orient Express? Why (not)?

Chapter 2

Before you read

8 Discuss these questions.

    a In this chapter, a dead body is discovered. Who do you think has been murdered?

    b What action will Poirot decide to take?

While you read

9 Complete the sentences with the correct words.

    a M. Bouc wants Poirot to solve the murder.

    b Mr Ratchett received threatening letters .

    c Mr Poirot thinks that Ratchett isn't his employer's real name.

    d Some of the wounds were made when Ratchett was already dead .

    e Daisy Armstrong was kidnapped and killed by Cassetti and his team of gangsters.

10 Which of these possible clues were found in Ratchett's compartment?

an open window   an empty glass   a knife   fingerprints
a handkerchief   a burnt note   money   a pocket watch
a gun   a pipe cleaner   a used match

11 Discuss the clues from activity 10. Describe them in as much detail as possible. What do you think they tell us about the murder?

12 Work in pairs. Have this conversation.

Student A: You are Michel, the train conductor. Tell M. Bouc about the dead body that you have discovered. You are very upset.

Student B: You are M. Bouc. Ask Michel questions about his discovery of a dead body. You are very upset.

13 What words are used to describe Ratchett/Cassetti? Do you feel at all sorry for him, or do you feel that his death was deserved? *Not good words, I don't feel sorry*

Chapter 3

Before you read

14 Do you think the murderer is still on the train? If you do, guess who it is. If you don't, guess how the murderer left the train. *Yes, the girl lc*

While you read

15 Complete the sentences with the correct times.

a Mr Ratchett's bell rang at .... *20:00* .

b Michel spoke to Mrs Hubbard and brought Poirot his water some time after .... *Poirot came* .

c Colonel Arbuthnot went to bed at about .... *10 pm* .

d The train stopped at Vincovci at .... *a gun* .

e Masterman last saw Ratchett at .... *11 pm* .

f Masterman went to sleep at about .... *3 hours* .

g The Swedish lady checked the bolt on Mrs Hubbard's door at .... *best* .

After you read

16 Why are these important in this chapter?
  a the door near the restaurant carriage *Some's leaving*
  b an Italian man *kH murder*
  c an aspirin
  d a metal button *Michael*
  e a red dressing gown *a woman*

17 Discuss the character and evidence of the people interviewed in this chapter. Could any of them be the murderer? Why (not)?

Chapter 4

Before you read

18 In this chapter, Poirot interviews five more passengers: the Swedish lady, Princess Dragomiroff, the Hungarian diplomat and his wife, and Colonel Arbuthnot. Guess which of them:
  a has a close connection with the Armstrong family. *Princess Dragomiroff*
  b smokes a pipe. *Colonel Arbuthnot*
  c has worked in the United States. *Hungarian diplomat*
  Now read and check your answers.

While you read

19 Complete the sentences with the correct names.
  a *Greta Ohlson* is sure that Miss Debenham stayed in her compartment all night.
  b *Princess Dragomiroff*'s maid came to her compartment and read to her.
  c Sonia Armstrong was the goddaughter of *Princess Dragomiroff*
  d There is an ink spot on the passport of *Countess Andreny*
  e *Countess Andreny* took medicine to help her sleep.
  f *Colonel Arbuthnot* saw someone looking out of his compartment door in a strange way.

After you read

20 Who is talking? Who are they talking about? Do you believe their words?
  a 'I remember reading about that. But I didn't know him.'
  Colonel Arbuthnot is talking about Robert Armstrong

b 'I believe she married an Englishman some years ago, but I'm afraid I cannot remember his name.'

c 'He and Ratchett probably worked in this kidnapping business together.'

d 'She can tell you nothing more than I have.'

21 Work in pairs. Have this conversation.

Student A: You are M. Bouc. Explain why you think that the Italian is the murderer, and why you disagree with Dr Constantine's ideas about the murder.

Student B: You are Dr Constantine. Explain why you disagree with M. Bouc, and give your own ideas about the murder.

Chapter 5

Before you read

22 There are four passengers left to interview: Miss Debenham, the Italian man, Princess Dragomiroff's maid, and the man in compartment 16. Guess the answers to these questions.

a Who will Poirot decide to interview next?

b Will any of them give evidence against another passenger?

c Who will Poirot think is most likely to be the murderer? Now read and check your answers.

While you read

23 Are these sentences true (T) or false (F)?

a Mr Hardman is really a salesman of office machines. F…..

b Mr Hardman saw a small, dark man in the corridor. F…..

c Mr Foscarelli likes to talk about his business. T…..

d Miss Debenham gives a lot of new information. F…..

e Michel almost ran into Hildegarde Schmidt after she had been in the Princess's compartment. F…..

After you read

24 Whose evidence suggests that:

a Masterman couldn't be the murderer? Foscarelli's

b the murderer couldn't be someone from another carriage of the train? *Hardman's*

c Ratchett was murdered by a stranger dressed in a conductor's uniform? *Hildegarde Schmidt's*

25 Do you believe all the evidence in activity 24? Why (not)?

Chapter 6

Before you read

26 Poirot has now interviewed all the passengers. What will he do next, do you think?

27 In this chapter, three important things are found. Can you guess what they are? Now read and check.

While you read

28 Put these events in the correct order, 1–6.

a Miss Debenham refuses to explain her words on the platform at Konya. *4*

b Mrs Hubbard screams. *1*

c Mrs Hubbard moves into a new compartment. *2*

d Hildegarde Schmidt suddenly becomes frightened. *5*

e Poirot looks inside his own suitcase. *6*

f Poirot notices a wet label on the Countess's luggage. *3*

After you read

29 Who or what do these words describe?

a 'we all agree that he exists' *the small dark man w/ a high voice*

b 'covered in dried blood' *the knife that Mrs Hubbard found in her sponge bag*

c 'showing no interest in the visitors' *Countess Andrenyi*

d 'in the pocket was a conductor's key' *conductor's uniform found in Hildegarde*

e 'she is still very upset' *Mrs. Hubbard*

f 'she showed signs of losing her temper' *Ms. Debenham*

30 Discuss the character of these passengers and any reasons for thinking they may be guilty.

a Miss Debenham

b Colonel Arbuthnot

c the Andrenyis

d Princess Dragomiroff

e Mrs Hubbard

31 If you were Poirot, what would you do to work out who the murderer is?

Chapter 7

Before you read

32 Work in groups of three and try to continue this conversation.

'Well,' said M. Bouc, 'this case makes no sense at all.'

'I agree,' said the doctor.

Poirot lit a cigarette. 'But the evidence of the passengers was very helpful.'

'I thought it told us nothing!' cried Bouc. 'What did I miss?'

33 Discuss these questions.

    a In this chapter, we discover that someone has been lying about their name. Can you guess who?

    b Who do you think the handkerchief really belongs to?

While you read

34 Write the names. Who:

    a is a member of Sonia Armstrong's family? ....

    b put an ink spot on a passport? ....

    c says she is the owner of the handkerchief? ....

After you read

35 Work in pairs. Have this conversation.

    Student A: You are Countess Andrenyi. Explain why you lied about your name.

    Student B: You are Poirot. Interview Countess Andrenyi and try to find out if she is the murderer.

36 Who do you now think murdered Ratchett? Explain your reasons.

Chapter 8

Before you read

37 In this chapter, Poirot uncovers more lies. Who else is lying, do you think?

38 What will happen at the end of the story, do you think? Will the murderer(s) be caught and sent to prison? Will they be sorry for their crime?

While you read

39 Make correct sentences.

a	Miss Debenham was	Helena's	nurse.
b	Foscarelli was	Robert Armstrong's	driver.
c	Greta Ohlsson was	the Armstrongs'	friend.
d	Michel is	Daisy's	father.
e	Colonel Arbuthnot was	Sonia and Helena's	governess.
f	Mrs Hubbard is	Susanne's	mother.

After you read

40 Did the solution of the crime come as a complete surprise to you, or had you guessed it? Which clues to the solution, if any, did you notice as you were reading?

41 Work in groups of three. You are three of the murderers on the day that Cassetti walked free from the court. Have a conversation about your feelings, and your plans for revenge.

42 Discuss these questions.

    a If you were the detective on the train, which of the two solutions would you give to the police? Why?

    b Do the murderers deserve punishment for their crime?

    c Is it ever right to take someone's life as punishment for a crime?

Writing

43 Write a newspaper article reporting the death of the Armstrongs' maid, Susanne, and the background to this event.

44 In the United States at the time of this story, murder was often punished by death. Discuss the similarities and differences between death through a court of law and Ratchett's death in this story.

45 Imagine that you are one of the murderers. Write a diary entry for the day that Cassetti walked free from the court.

46 Imagine that you are Miss Debenham or Mr MacQueen. It is several months before your journey on the Orient Express begins. Write a letter to one of the other murderers, giving instructions and details of your murder plans.

47 Although Hercule Poirot was Agatha Christie's most famous character, she was not very fond of him. What are his good qualities and his faults?

48 Describe the most interesting passenger on the train. Why does this person interest you?

49 Is Agatha Christie fair to her readers? Does she give them enough clues to solve the crime before Poirot's explanation at the end?

50 Do you think you would enjoy being a passenger on the Orient Express at the time of the story? Think about both the richer passengers and the servants.

51 In what ways is *Murder on the Orient Express* a now-typical murder mystery story? In what ways does it break the rules of this type of story?

52 What do you think are the reasons for the story's continuing popularity?

WORD LIST

aspirin (n) medicine that reduces pain and fever

bolt (n/v) a piece of metal that you push across a door so it cannot be opened

carriage (n) one of the connected parts of a train, where passengers sit

case (n) a crime or other mystery that a detective works on

clue (n) something that helps to solve a mystery

colonel (n) someone with a high position in the army

compartment (n) one of the separated parts of a carriage, used for sitting in and, on a long-distance train, often as a bedroom

conductor (n) someone who checks tickets and looks after passengers on a train

corridor (n) a long, narrow space with doors leading off it

count/countess (n) a man/woman from an upper-class family

curl (v) to bend into a round shape

diplomat (n) someone who works for their country's government in a foreign country

dressing gown (n) a long, loose coat, usually worn inside your own house

efficient (adj) working well without wasting time or energy

evidence (n) information that makes you believe something

evil (n/adj) behaviour that is very, very bad and/or intentionally harmful to others

express (n) a train that travels very quickly

goddaughter (n) a girl with whom you have a special relationship as a result of a choice by the girl's actual parents when the girl is very young

governess (n) a female teacher who lives with a rich family

label (n) a piece of paper that is stuck or tied onto something and gives information about it

maid (n) a female servant

novel (n) a long, written story about fictional characters

pipe (n) something that is used for smoking tobacco, with a thin tube at one end and a small bowl for the tobacco at the other; a **pipe cleaner** is pushed along the inside of a pipe to clean it

pyjamas (n) trousers and a top that you wear in bed

reputation (n) the opinions that people have of someone

revenge (n) something done to punish someone who has harmed you

sponge bag (n) a small bag for the things that you need in the bathroom

threaten (v) to say that you will cause harm to someone

wire (n) a thin string of metal; **wire netting** is made of wires fixed across each other with regular spaces between them

wound (n) a cut or hole in your skin, often caused by a knife or gun